'A Scottish W Odyssey'

In Search of Scotland's Wild Secrets

Keith Broomfield

With Illustrations by

Rob Hands

TIPPERMUIR
· BOOKS LIMITED ·

This first edition published and copyright 2022 by
Tippermuir Books Ltd, Perth, Scotland.
mail@tippermuirbooks.co.uk www.tippermuirbooks.co.uk.

ISBN 978-1-913836-13-9 (paperback)

A CIP catalogue record for this book is available from the British Library.

Editorial and Project coordination by Dr Paul S Philippou.

Cover design by Matthew Mackie.
Editorial support: Jean Hands, Allan Laing and Steve Zajda.
Map/Illustrations by Rob Hands.

Text design, layout, and artwork by Bernard Chandler [graffik].
Text set in Dante MT Std 10.5/14pt.

Printed and Bound by Ashford Colour Press Ltd, Gosport PO13 0FW

To My Children
Laura and Ross

ACKNOWLEDGEMENTS

Special thanks to Paul Philippou of Tippermuir Books for providing the original idea for *A Scottish Wildlife Odyssey* and for his support throughout the writing and production process. I am also indebted to Rob Hands for his wonderful illustrations, Matthew Mackie for yet another great cover, Jean Hands and Steve Zajda for their careful proof reading and Bernard Chandler for his expertise in graphical design and typesetting.

Thanks also to Professor Colin Bean of ScotNature for his input on vendace, Jack Wootton and Scot Muir of Forth Rivers Trust for their help on eels, Cath Scott, Natural Environment Officer for Glasgow City Council, for her water vole contribution, Gwendolyn Raes of Woodland Trust Scotland for her support in the Glen Finglas chapter, Alison and Angus McGregor for inviting me to Skye, and to Ashley Hose, Alan Armstrong and Pauline Parandian for their advice on Shetland. Finally, many thanks to my wife, Lynda, for her continued support and encouragement for my book writing endeavours

During the research and writing of this book, changing Covid-19 restrictions were imposed in Scotland. Advice from the Scottish Government was sought on travel during this period, with which there was full compliance.

CONTENTS

Prologue

UNDER A WHISPERING BREEZE

Under a whispering breeze on the cold rocky autumnal shore at Waternish in the far north of Skye, I witnessed a dawning that quickly gathered momentum, a transformation from the subliminal into the consciousness. Artists and photographers, and probably most other people too, have long known this, but the realisation fell upon me that it was the infinite diversity of light that gives Scotland such a special ambience. It was a revelatory moment, for the range and variance of these subtle lustres had not struck home in any meaningful way before. As I gazed out across the Minch towards the brooding hills of Harris, the silvery sea sparkled and danced in a quite remarkable way. It was a catalyst, an arousal of the mind, that sparked me to look upon this panorama in a more analytical way.

Squally rain clouds hurtled across the heavens, intermittently blocking the sunshine, and turning the water ashen. Then the sun quickly reappeared, and the sea twinkled once more. This was an environment of a myriad hues and wild reflections.

An arcing rainbow of dazzling colour materialised out towards Waternish Point and just as swiftly faded. On the far side of Loch Dunvegan, the hills were veiled in a translucent haze before clearing under the brightness of the light. It was an alternating vista of sun and rain, cloud and mist – and it was truly magical.

Sheer contentment swept across my soul on this remote rock-strewn shore, my wetsuit clad body still dripping after having emerged from the sea. I had just been snorkelling, during which I had become part of another ever-changing world, glimpsing shoals of young saithe gliding over the kelp forests and watching rock cook and ballan wrasse flicker between their broad, green fronds. The saucer-shaped form of a crystal jellyfish had pulsed past me like a beating heart and pink-tinted starfish clung to underwater rock faces.

The water visibility was gin clear, but it was well into October 2020, and with the lateness of the season, I knew this would probably be my last snorkel of the year. As such, I had stayed in the water for as long as the cold would permit, totally absorbed by this undersea tapestry of life and colour.

Such marine riches are often a forgotten part of Scotland's wild nature, yet, it is the sea which is one of the driving forces that define the country's environment. Situated on the north western periphery of Europe, the warming influences of the perpetual oceanic current known as the North Atlantic Drift (also called the North Atlantic Current or Gulf Stream), combined with prevailing south-westerly winds, helps keep Scotland's climate benign compared to other areas of the world at similar latitudes. For birds such as geese and waders that breed in the Arctic and sub-Arctic, Scotland is the perfect migratory staging post and wintering ground, offering verdant fields for grazing geese, and sheltered firths and estuaries where waders can probe for their rich invertebrate life.

Towering sea cliffs on both Atlantic and North Sea coasts are havens for nesting sea birds such as puffins and guillemots, and tumbling rivers are home to spawning salmon. Scotland is at the interface of where north meets south, a place for summer visiting warblers and swallows from Africa to breed, and home to icy relics from the north such as ptarmigan and snow buntings. Scotland is incredibly diverse in its physical geography, with mountains over 1,200 m, large coastal plains on the east coast and a myriad of islands in the west and north. There are woodlands and lochs, heather moors and vast bogs, rich agricultural land and deep penetrating firths. It is hard to imagine how there could be so much landscape variation over such a small area.

The calming hand of the sea and warming winds are there all the time, ensuring that, in the main, Scotland is not a land of extremes. There is no penetrating cold nor searing heat. Instead, Scotland is a wet and mild place where a multitude of creatures and plants prosper. There are exceptions. On the high mountain tops in winter, the temperature can plummet to create a harsh, freezing arctic-alpine environment. Even at lower levels, snow can carpet the ground for weeks at a time.

On a personal level, Scotland has delivered many nature memories: finding my first dotterel on a whaleback ridge in the Cairngorms, the awe of seeing the dark triangular fin of a large basking shark breaking the water in the Firth of Clyde and spotting a golden eagle eyrie in a remote Deeside glen. I have so many recollections that as I considered them, they fell upon my mind in rapid succession: the floral splendour of the Hebridean machair in June, being dive-bombed by an angry bonxie in Shetland and the cacophony of swirling noise from gannets on the guano-covered Bass Rock. The list goes on.

There is, however, much more to Scotland's nature than what might be perceived as the dramatic, and here I am thinking of the joys of guddling around rockpools on the Angus coast, watching foxes in suburban Edinburgh or searching for fungi in a birch wood in the Forest of Birse in Aberdeenshire.

Indeed, such 'normal' wild experiences are in many ways what I adore most about Scotland, for they encapsulate my inner interest in nature. It was such local reflections that led me to write *If Rivers Could Sing* (2020), a wildlife journey on my home river, the Devon, which flows through Perthshire, Kinross-shire and Clackmannanshire. Following its publication, I was keen to write another book focusing on the nature of another small part of Scotland, for I like to delve deep and to get to know an area intimately. Tippermuir Books' publisher Paul Philippou persuaded me otherwise. Be more expansive, he suggested. Why not go on a Scottish wildlife journey and turn that into a book?

I wasn't sure at first, for that seemed a bit daunting, but then the memories came flooding back: those wonderful times in Shetland, the days spent walking the rounded tops of the Monadhliath Mountains or ambling along the Berwickshire coast in search of grey seals. That would certainly be nice to do again. Besides, there were numerous other parts of Scotland that I had yet to visit. A Scottish wildlife journey – yes, it did feel compelling, and this seed corn of an idea soon germinated into a powerful burning force.

And so, starting from Dumfries and Galloway in the south-west, I embarked upon this Scottish nature odyssey, zig-zagging my way across and up through Scotland, alternating between west and east, heading northwards all the while, until the trip end in Shetland. This five-month journey was in no way comprehensive, more a snapshot of Scottish nature, a random dip into its deep richness. This is a journey that could be completed a thousand times, and on each occasion a different route could be taken that would unveil its own unique wildlife surprises.

My intention was to visit some well-known places, but also the lesser frequented, because no matter where you go in Scotland, there is something wonderful to see. After all, that is the nature of Scotland and the lifeblood that makes this wild land on the Atlantic edge so special.

———————————————

Chapter 1

DAWN ON THE CAERLAVEROCK MERSE

March 2021 – Solway Firth

As dawn broke to reveal the frost-glistened air, a low haar on the horizon crept across the distant margins of the open flatlands of the merse. Above this grey-blurred blanket of hazy sea mist, a pink shimmer glowed and flickered. The sun was slowly rising, and nature was beginning to stir.

The vast emptiness of the merse at Caerlaverock on the fringes of the Solway Firth had taken me by surprise and its captivating hold was overwhelming. This is quite unlike any other place I have visited in Scotland. It is a pancake-flat saltmarsh that stretches as far as the eye can see. Its appearance is akin to the Arctic tundra, with its short-cropped grasses and random scattering of pools. The reality is more benign. The merse is a gentle, pleasant place, with a wild soul. Its natural spell was all-encompassing – an environ of open skies and a sanctuary of reflection.

Merse – a local term for saltmarsh – is a wonderful name that trips easily off the tongue in a manner that is both poetic and descriptive. Despite the white-sparkled frost, the rich song of a skylark abruptly cascaded down from above. With squinting eyes, I scanned the heavens but there was no sign of the lark. Then, as if by mysterious magic, he materialised, rising higher and higher on quivering wings, the head moving from side to side as he let drip his sweet-tempered notes. I have noticed this constant turning of the head with singing skylarks before; an effective ploy for spraying their sweet music over the widest possible area.

In spring, skylarks often sing just before dawn, giving rise to the familiar saying 'rising with the lark'. The compelling beauty of their song has been revered by poets over many centuries. William Wordsworth penned his tribute, 'To a Skylark', in 1815:

There is a madness about thee, and joy divine,
In that song of thine;
Lift me, guide me high and high,
To thy banqueting place in the sky.

Skylark

My singing skylark had reinvigorated my spirit in a way that few other birds ever could, fuelling anticipation for seeking out my main quarry, barnacle geese. I knew they were about because on arrival under the cover of darkness, their constant high-pitched yelping cries floated across the ice-pinched air, albeit from some distance away.

As the dawn gathered pace, the first barnacle geese appeared, mostly in small flights, comprising of a handful of birds swooping low over the tidal saltmarsh. I was still on the landward edge of the merse, so I followed a narrow path used by wildfowlers and headed deep within its salt-breezed embrace. I followed a muddy channel that cut through the merse as it ran its way down towards the Solway Firth. Although the ground underfoot was firm, the going was rough, as I constantly negotiated routes across other watery channels that bisected the landscape. The tide was out, and these steep-banked ditches oozed with dark, clawing mud.

Redshanks intermittently rose into the air before me, their piping calls forewarning of my approach. These small greyish waders, with long red legs, are part of the wild beating heart of Scottish coasts during winter and are ever-constant companions, no matter the harshness of the weather.

Suddenly, I heard an abrupt clanging clamour from the west as the sky erupted into a black-speckled explosion as a multitude of barnacle geese took to the air. The geese were perhaps a kilometre away and had previously been resting on the ground out of my view. At the behest of an unknown cue, they had taken instant flight and were heading towards me. It was hard to be sure, but there must have been almost a thousand of them, a clamouring throng of vibrant life.

Barnacle Geese (Caerlaverock)

The huge skein split into two, and on measured wings, they rapidly approached, one flock veering to the north of me, the other staying on the seaward side. Their wild echoes were mesmerising, and in the starkness of this open merse, it felt as if I had merged into the being of the landscape. An instant wave of euphoria swept over me, instilling a groundswell of inner emotion that only nature can deliver.

The geese passed by, and on whiffling wings alighted on a mudbank close to the firth, calling all the while. Once they had settled, their murmurings quietened. They had hunkered down to rest.

I scrutinised the barnacles through my binoculars and was struck by the subtle beauty of their white faces, black caps and necks, and grey-barred plumage. They are smaller and dumpier than the commoner and more widespread greylag and pink-footed geese that also winter in Scotland. After breeding in the Svalbard (Spitzbergen) archipelago, between Norway and the North Pole, the entire population of around 40,000 birds sets off for the Solway in late August, arriving in September. They stay until April when they embark upon their marathon return migration.

On watching them, I reflected upon the importance of the saltmarshes and mudflats of the Solway Firth to this population. What would have happened to them if in modern times these saltmarshes had been reclaimed for agriculture or other development? It doesn't bear thinking about. Such is the fragility of nature and our power to destroy it.

Barnacle geese would have been making this migration between Svalbard and the south-west of Scotland for thousands of years. Without this safe winter sanctuary their numbers would surely have dwindled, perhaps even to the point of extinction. A further question arose in my mind: How did the evolutionary processes of this epic barnacle goose migration unfold? The more you think, the less you understand. Maybe it is better just to appreciate the beauty of these geese, rather than to philosophise on the incomprehensible.

My thoughts buzzed with images of the far northern Arctic islands where barnacle geese breed, a land that is home to Arctic foxes and polar bears. Arctic foxes are an ever-present threat to the barnacles' eggs and goslings, and to avoid predation, the geese often nest on cliff ledges. When the youngsters are just three days old and nowhere near being able to fly, they make a death-defying leap to the flat grasslands below. Many are dashed against rocks and perish before they have even had a chance to live, their bodies eagerly devoured by foxes prowling below.

Humans have been intrigued by barnacle geese since the earliest of times, with the origins of wintering birds causing much head-scratching, given that their nests had never been found and migration was a phenomenon not understood. As such, their peculiar name arose from the belief that the birds hatched from barnacles growing on driftwood.

Interestingly, there is another separate population of barnacle geese that breeds in Greenland and which winters in northern and western parts of Scotland, extending from Orkney and down through the numerous islands of the Outer and Inner Hebrides to Islay. These two distinct populations remain discrete in both their breeding and winter populations, and never the twain do meet. They do, however, have one thing in common: a dependence on Scotland as a place to escape from the cruel harshness of the Arctic winter.

After watching the geese for several minutes, I wandered further down the edge of the main water channel to where the saltmarsh meets the open mudflats and sandbanks of the Solway. Groups of shelduck huddled by the merse edge, where the vast expanse of intertidal mud and sand swept out as far as the eye could see, disappearing into the grey wispy ebb of haar where the Cumbrian coast of England lay hidden only a handful of kilometres away.

I took a tentative step out onto the open mud. My boots sank up to my ankles and so I beat a hasty retreat. It would be foolhardy to venture any further, for the Solway is infamous for its quicksands, huge tidal range and unpredictable currents, and this was not a place to become stuck. Such is the power and turmoil of the tides and currents that the merse never stands still, continually eroding in some areas and extending in others. It is a moving, dynamic landscape, a place that nature continually sculpts.

Saltmarsh is part land and part water, exposed to the air for much of the time and flooded by the highest tides. It is a peculiarly unique habitat and home to a range of specially adapted salt-tolerant plants such as marsh samphire, sea blight and holy grass. Marsh samphire (also known as glasswort) is an intriguing plant, that sports the fleshy shape and form of a small cactus, but without the prickly spines. When the first pioneer plants such as samphire gain a foothold in the mud by the sea edge, they trap silt in among their roots and stems, stabilising the ground and enabling other species such as sea spurrey to colonise.

The Solway holds around a quarter of all saltmarsh found in the UK, and Caerlaverock, which is a national nature reserve, boasts the largest continuous area of merse in Scotland. Out in the mud and sand of the firth, even more life abounds, including marine molluscs such as cockles, snails and tellins, as well as mud shrimps. This abundance of invertebrate life in turn attracts up to 140,000 wintering wildfowl and waders, including pintail ducks, knots, oystercatchers, bar-tailed godwits and curlews. The Solway is a place of immense international importance for wildlife, a haven where its vast expanse of water, land, and that blurred area that lies somewhere in between, provides shelter and food. Saltmarshes are crucial carbon sinks, and as such, are places to be cherished and revered.

Having abandoned the idea of wandering further out onto the mud towards the sea, I began instead to explore the shallow channels that cut through the merse. On the muddy banks that lined each deep cut, a proliferation of the first early-spring emergence of scurvygrass grew. Despite the name, this is not a grass at all, but a flowering plant that thrives on saltmarshes and other coastal areas. Scurvygrass features distinctive flattened, ivy-shaped leaves that are rich in Vitamin C, and which in times past were widely used in the prevention of scurvy aboard sailing ships.

I found it hard to comprehend how this scurvygrass could prosper in an environment where it is regularly submerged by the brackish tide until realising the watery inundation brings with it a rich cocktail of nutrients, enabling such plants to thrive. On making my way across the merse, hopping with caution across each channel lest I should slip, numerous fragments of bladder wrack seaweed scattered the ground, discarded by the high tides, and acting as a reminder that the influence of the sea is all pervasive in this vast, open landscape.

At the bottom of another channel, silt billowed out from a tiny underwater hole in the mud which at first glance appeared to be home to a type of worm that was filter feeding. I stooped down to investigate, intrigued by the clouds of sediment streaming like smoke from the mouth of its burrow. I quickly changed my mind. Perhaps this was not a worm after all and possibly a crustacean, I thought, for I occasionally glimpsed what looked like two tentacles at the hole entrance, leaving me frustrated at my inability to identify the creature held within. It was just one more natural secret of the merse, which added to its special aura.

It was hard to draw away from this unusually dramatic place, but I was keen to explore more of the Solway Firth, and on my return to the nature reserve car park, I passed several shallow pools on the landward side of the merse where I suspected natterjack toads might breed. This was early March and it would not be until the following month that they would emerge from hibernation and start to spawn. Natterjacks are Scotland's rarest amphibian and are on the extreme edge of their geographical range on the Solway. The natterjack is similar in appearance to the common toad, but it is smaller, runs rather than leaps, and has a distinctive yellow stripe running down the back.

The scarcity of natterjacks is due to their fussy requirements of preferring areas of shallow pools on sand-dunes, heaths and marshes. The shallow pools at Caerlaverock are ideal for their needs, drying out in the summer and occasionally flushed with seawater from extreme high tides, preventing predators such as fish and aquatic invertebrates from colonising the pools and eating their eggs and tadpoles.

My next stop was the attractive hamlet of Rockcliffe that lies about 20 km further westwards along the Solway Firth. Here, a scattered cluster of imposing houses looks across the tidal inlet known as Rough Firth. Out on the exposed mud of the firth, small groups of curlews and oystercatchers dabbled, their long bills probing the ooze for worms and molluscs.

I trod carefully down to the foreshore, scrambling over a band of rocks that edged the flank of this small tributary firth, which was part of the estuary of the Urr Water. On the margin that lay between mud and the shoreside rock, I was astonished to discover a huge congregation of cockles. It is not unusual to find remnant half-shells of cockles on the seashore, but this was different, for these were whole-shelled, living animals. I scooped my hands among their mass and lifted some out. They were the size of large grey-brown marbles, each shell engraved with radiating ribs.

Live cockles are seldom seen because they bury themselves in the sand and mud and feed by siphoning and filtering water to glean microscopic plankton. Presumably, gales and rough seas the previous week had dislodged these cockles from their subsurface homes and scattered them along the foreshore.

For a mollusc, cockles are surprisingly mobile, and in time, most of these animals will move and dig themselves back under the sand by using a specially adapted 'foot'. This abundance of cockles underlined the vast reservoir of marine life held within the muddy gloop of the Solway. Estuarine mud is like a protein soup, hugely productive and a powerhouse that supports so much else.

Coastal sand and mud habitats by the coast may lack the diversity of species found on rocky shores, but this is more than compensated by the sheer abundance of those that live within this hidden environment. Sand creatures, such as cockles, thrive in one of the toughest places imaginable, continually pounded by wild storms and scoured by surging tidal currents. They are true survivors.

Later that morning, I travelled north-westwards, heading through the small market town of Castle Douglas and onto Loch Ken, a sparkling slender sliver of fresh water that stretches for some 16 km and is fringed with swamp, fen, marsh and woodland.

The frost-laden dawn on the Solway had now transformed into a wonderful sunny day. Early March is such a special time, for it is the overlap between winter and spring, and as I ambled down a track at the RSPB Ken-Dee Marshes Reserve, flocks of fieldfares cackled noisily and bounded through the air, no doubt aware that they would soon be heading to their breeding grounds in Scandinavia.

In a field close to the water's edge, a small group of grey geese lingered, which brought me excitedly fumbling for my binoculars, for another rare goose species occurs in this part of country – the Greenland white-fronted goose. These scarce geese arrive from Greenland in early October and this population (there are others that visit other parts of Scotland) peak at around 350 birds by mid-November, before departing back to the Arctic in April.

Greenland white-fronts are similar to the more common greylag goose but are slightly smaller and have a distinctive white band around the base of the bill. I scanned the flock, examining each bird with mounting anticipation, but all the birds were greylags. A twinge of disappointment, which soon dissipated, for watching these greylags quietly grazing under the spring sun was soothing. Does it matter whether a creature is rare or common when appreciating shape or form? No, of course not, for the compulsion to see something rare is more an aberration of the mind rather than a reflection of reality.

Not long after, a red kite floated into view, plying the subtle air currents on splayed wings and using casual flicks of its deeply forked tail to give direction and purpose. It was a most elegant bird of prey, with the long wings and slender body delivering an impression of underlying fragility. This kite was inquisitive, and it purposefully glided towards me before swirling above in large circles, its pale head and deep yellow piercing eyes catching the early spring sun.

Such an inspiring sight would have been unthinkable only a few decades previously. As a young nature enthusiast growing up in the 1970s, my well-thumbed Collins bird guidebook described the red kite as one of our scarcest birds of prey, with only a handful of pairs hanging on in the remote Welsh valleys. In times past, the kite was widely spread throughout Scotland, even scavenging for rubbish in the streets of Edinburgh. The typical gliding flight lent the old name for the bird – glead or gled, derivations of which can still be found in place names today such as Gladhouse and Gledhill. In an Act of James II in 1457, gleds were mentioned amongst birds of prey which should be destroyed, and by the end of the nineteenth century the intensity of persecution had become such that it had been wiped out from Scotland altogether.

Red Kite (Ken-Dee Marshes)

Thankfully, all was not lost, and pioneering reintroduction schemes using young birds from other parts of Europe began in the 1990s, first on the Black Isle north of Inverness and then near Doune in central Scotland, followed by Galloway and Aberdeenshire, which dramatically turned around their fortunes.

Kites are handsome raptors that have been sorely missed and it seems entirely appropriate that the hand that brought their demise has in these more enlightened times been responsible for a quite remarkable resurrection.

Such has been the success of the Galloway reintroduction scheme that kites are now a frequent sight when driving through the area. As well as the ecological dividend of having these birds back where they belong, they bring economic benefits too, including the creation of the Galloway

Red Kite Trail. This tourist trail is a suggested route which has been designed to provide good opportunities to see red kites in Galloway. It is a concept I find appealing. Nature is the oxygen of life. When it is also recognised as an economic asset that provides discernible benefit, we are so much more likely to look after it.

Soon, I was down upon the water by the shore of Loch Ken, where small groups of teal and mallards bobbed, and on the far side of the water a herd of whooper swans glided. These elegant winter-visiting whoopers brought back fond memories of previous encounters, especially the excitement of watching an incoming family flight. As nature encounters go, there is nothing quite like it. They swoop in with their long necks extended, the air thrumming from the rhythmic swish of powerful wings digging deep into the cold winter air. The perfect formation makes a final bank before descending upon the water's surface, which erupts into a trailing splatter of spume as the swans abruptly come to rest.

My final destination was Castramon Wood, a Scottish Wildlife Trust reserve. Lying to the north of Gatehouse of Fleet, and nestled in the folds of the Galloway Hills, Castramon is one of the largest semi-natural broadleaved woodlands in the area. Its oak trees were once used for making charcoal and supplying the local mill with bobbins. Nowadays, the trees provide lush conditions for ferns and lichens.

It is a serene and beguiling place, and in a woodland clearing I sat on a fallen tree trunk, where nearby hazel catkins gently swayed in the breeze. These catkins are also known as 'lambs' tails' – a most appropriate name. More a bush than a tree, the hazel is a fundamental keystone of our countryside yet so often overlooked because for much of the year it is rather inconspicuous. Yet all this changes in early spring when their hanging lime-coloured catkins decorate the branches like shiny baubles on a Christmas tree. It is as much a sign of the new season of life as frog spawn or early emerging daffodils. These dangly catkins are the male flowers but look closer at the branches and the tiny bud-like red female flowers can be seen too. Pollinated by the wind, by autumn these will have developed into small hazelnut clusters.

By my feet, the first early green shoots of bluebells were emerging, and in a couple of months this woodland would become a blue-buzzed haze, a place where scarce summer-visiting songbirds such as pied flycatchers and redstarts breed. The sharp, whistling call of a nuthatch suddenly spun through the air. About the size of a plump sparrow, the attractive plumage of a nuthatch is a smooth mix of slate-grey, buff and chestnut. The piercing song catches the attention in a way few other bird calls do: a liquid-flowing repertoire fit for any choir, with an incredible range of ringing notes including one melody that sounds like a boy whistling. The poet, John Clare, described the song as a 'long and loud continued noise' that 'often stops the speed of men and boys'.

The nuthatch looks like a small dumpy woodpecker, but unlike a woodpecker it can crawl down a tree trunk headfirst, its sharp grasping claws providing perfect grip and its long bill ideal for searching the nooks and crannies of the bark for insects. A few decades ago, nuthatches had only been sparingly recorded in Scotland, despite being a common breeding bird in England. Then, in the 1980s, something remarkable happened: the number of records increased, and the first breeding occurred in the Scottish Borders. The nuthatch has spread rapidly ever since and is now well established in many southern and central parts of Scotland.

Nuthatches are surprisingly difficult birds to see but, by chance, I caught sight of this one high on the bough of an oak, where it scrutinised meticulously the wrinkled bark with its powerful bill, before flying away and vanishing in among the thick tangle of branches. It was a good sighting and as I sat on the tumbled tree trunk, life felt as good as it has ever been. The sun shone and the air was warm, and it was wonderfully relaxing to be within the welcoming clutch of the wood. Sadness ebbed in too, for it was time to go and my visit to this south-western corner of Scotland was nearing an end.

I had only just embarked upon my Scottish nature journey and already a wide range of emotions brimmed upon my consciousness. I felt enthused and enthralled in equal measure at the rich variety of wildness that had unfolded before my eyes. This is an oft-forgotten part of Scotland, but within its compass lies stunning merse lands and coastal scenery, rolling hills, and verdant forests and fields. It is an area where surprises abound at every turn. Moreover, it is a place with an addictive quality, where one could spend a lifetime exploring its wild secrets, questioning and fathoming, but never finding all the answers.

Chapter 2

WILD GOATS AND ENDANGERED FISH

March 2021 – Moffat Hills and the River Tweed

The humble vendace was once a common staple of the good folk of Lochmaben, which lies a few miles to the west of Lockerbie in Dumfries and Galloway. They even held special parties in celebration of their esteem for this small herring-like fish that in times past swam in abundance in the nearby Mill and Castle Lochs, but which today is one of Scotland's rarest and most endangered freshwater fish.

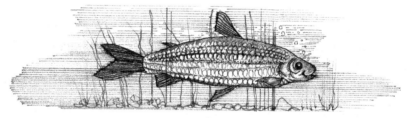

Vendace

Due to deterioration in water quality combined with the impact of non-native water plants and fish, the vendace disappeared from Castle Loch in the first half of the twentieth century and Mill Loch in the early 1970s, the only sites in Scotland where these silvery plankton-eating fish occurred. It is said that Mary Queen of Scots brought vendace to these lochs from Europe in 1565, but this is no more than a fanciful yarn, for in reality it is one of the few freshwater fish that managed to colonise Britain at the end of the last Ice Age.

This Scotland extinction sparked into action a remarkable rescue programme. In the mid-1990s, an action plan, co-ordinated by Scottish Natural Heritage (now NatureScot) and the Environment Agency in England, was launched to create refuge sites for vendace utilising the two surviving indigenous UK populations that were still hanging on just across the border in the Lake District at Derwent Water and Bassenthwaite.

Under this species recovery plan, fertilised vendace eggs and small fry from Bassenthwaite were introduced into Loch Skeen, near Moffat in Dumfriesshire, as a safe sanctuary to hold these valuable fish. This introduction proved even more important, given that the population in Bassenthwaite was perilously small. Indeed, it was thought the Bassenthwaite fish had even become extinct by 2012, although vendace have occasionally been caught there since then. This genetically unique population had been given a crucial helping hand with the fish safely holed up at Loch Skeen and subsequently breeding successfully.

On the next stage of my Scottish nature odyssey, I found myself standing by the edge of this remarkable fish refuge at Loch Skeen high in the Moffat Hills, above the famous Grey Mare's Tail hanging valley waterfall. With a bit of imagination, the falls, which are the fifth highest in the UK, do indeed bear a passing equine resemblance, with their long, white-flecked cascades flickering like a horse's tail on the gallop. A National Trust for Scotland reserve, the steep ascent on a hill flank beside the waterfall is along a well-maintained and steep path. I had been to the Grey Mare's Tail several times before, and normally the panorama is inspiring, but on that early March morning, thick, swirling mist enveloped the hills and my glasses continually steamed up.

A *cronking* raven swept past on black-cloaked wings, disappearing into the grey, wispy mist as quickly as it had appeared. Peregrine falcons haunt this area, but I knew that on such a miserable day there was little chance of seeing one as they would be lying low due to the difficult hunting conditions. As ever in these parts, sheep were abundant, and then, in among the sheep, I spotted something more unusual – a feral goat and her young kid.

The mother (nanny goat) sported small, short, gently curved horns and a long, shaggy, black and white coat. She continuously nibbled the short-cropped vegetation paying scant attention to my near presence. The kid, which was also black and white furred, looked only a few weeks old and was undeniably attractive as all young animals are.

The first goats arrived in the British Isles as domestic stock in Neolithic times, and the feral animals that live in the Grey Mare's Tail area and other parts of the Southern Uplands have been around since at least the nineteenth

Feral Goats (Loch Skeen)

century, originating as escapees or perhaps deliberate releases. Present day feral goats often show characteristics of old domestic breeds.

While naturalised, they cannot, in any sense of the word, be described as native, especially since they bring unwelcome additional pressures to these already heavily sheep-grazed hills. Indeed, the outlook of these hills, and those in many other parts of Scotland, is not natural at all. It is a much diminished and denuded environment that lacks biodiversity and vibrancy because of intensive grazing. Prior to the impact of people, much of these hills were wild-forested with a range of native species, including oak, birch and aspen. The clearings would have been bursting with wildflowers that were continually buzzed by bees and other insects.

As I wandered up the path towards Loch Skeen, my inescapable conclusion was that utilising vast, blanket tracts of open hill for sheep to roam is an unsustainable form of land use and food production. We rightly cherish farmers for the food they produce, along with the spin-off employment created in rural areas, but this inevitably creates an environmental footprint – any form of human activity does and that is inescapable.

There must be, however, a better way for sustainable management on marginal land, which maintains profitable food production at current levels whilst also rewilding parts of the landscape, benefiting farmers, wider society and nature. At the very least, a network of small reserve areas, free from agricultural grazing, would deliver both economic and ecological dividends. In the simplest terms, it is all down to a matter of fencing, so than rather than having vast hill areas where sheep roam at will, the creation of a network of fenced-off areas would provide protected areas for native flora and fauna to prosper, without impacting upon sheep numbers in any given area.

Creating a patchwork of protected wild areas in overgrazed landscapes would benefit biodiversity, restore nature and tackle climate breakdown, without impinging upon food production levels and livelihoods. Rewilding has the potential to deliver additional rural employment through a variety of other activities, including outdoor recreation.

Such adaptive and gradual changes in land use, if ever brought to fruition, should not be delivered by diktat and compulsion, but instead voluntarily through incentives, for that is a moral and effective way to achieve such goals. Some might say that this is a pie-in-the-sky vision, but these are issues that should be debated and discussed, for the future of humanity depends upon a sea change in thinking on how we manage our resources.

This impact of overgrazing was brought home to me when I reached Loch Skeen, for on a tiny rocky island just metres out on the water, a lone wind-sculpted birch gained tenure, crowned with a crow's nest held within the confines of its twisted branches. Safe from grazing sheep and goats, this was the only place where this tree could survive – a lone sentinel reminder of the environmental issues we face.

On my final approach to Loch Skeen, moraines – rounded hummocks of glacial deposits comprising silt, pebbles, and boulders – dotted the landscape. The mist and low cloud lifted intermittently, revealing the impressive, steep-curved top of White Coomb, which at 821m is Dumfriesshire's highest hill. The summit of White Coomb holds burial cairns around 3,500 to 4,000 years old.

As I stood on the shore edge of this high loch, my thoughts turned once more to the endangered vendace that lay beneath the water. Since this pioneering species recovery project begun, vendace have been introduced to three other water bodies to act as refuges: Loch Earn in Perthshire, Daer Reservoir in South Lanarkshire and Loch Valley in Galloway.

The similarly threatened powan, a close cousin of the vendace whose natural distribution in Scotland is restricted to Loch Lomond and Loch Eck, has also been given a helping hand with successful introductions having been made at several sites in central Scotland and Argyll. Such introduction schemes play a vital role in ensuring that our precious diversity of freshwater fish life is not lost.

The same principle applies to birds such as the Galloway red kites which I had only so recently encountered, and another ambitious recovery programme is under way to enhance the local golden eagle population. At a secret location in the Moffat Hills, possibly somewhere near where Loch Skeen nestles, eagles are being reintroduced. Since 2018, the South of Scotland Golden Eagle Project has successfully translocated several young golden eagles from the Scottish Highlands to the south of Scotland, with more due to follow. Before the project began, there were only a few pairs of golden eagles across Dumfries and Galloway and the Scottish Borders. A support study by NatureScot showed that the local habitat is suitable for up to 16 pairs. It is a tantalising prospect to have healthy populations of golden eagles soaring once more over much of their former home range in the Southern Uplands.

Following my thought-provoking visit to the Grey Mare's Tail and Loch Skeen, I headed towards Peebles and the River Tweed, passing St Mary's Loch, where small groups of winter-visiting goldeneye ducks swam and dived out on the water.

Starting from Kingsmeadows Road car park in Peebles, which lies in the shadow of the Tweed Bridge, I walked upstream along the southern bank of the river. The previous mist and drizzle that shrouded the Moffat Hills had now cleared and a smooth, warming, early spring sun had taken hold. The River Tweed is famous for its trout and salmon, and another intriguing fish – the grayling – also haunts its watery embrace.

Graylings are widespread in Europe, but in Scotland are confined to central and southern rivers, including the Tweed. The grayling is not native to Scotland, having been first introduced to the River Clyde from England in the nineteenth century, followed by several other rivers, and are a much-prized quarry of anglers.

I recall catching grayling when fly-fishing in Slovenia several years previously. They were strong fighting fish, and on landing, displayed a resplendent sail-like dorsal fin (top-fin). Graylings are sometimes known as the 'lady-of-the-stream', which seems an entirely apt description for such an elegant fish. Like the feral goats of the Moffat Hills, they are just one more example of the plethora of introduced species which inhabit Scotland.

Peregrine Falcon (Neidpath Viaduct)

I wandered further along the south bank of the Tweed as far as the Neidpath railway viaduct, which opened in 1864 as part of the Peebles to Symington branch line. The walk was pleasant, with the flow of the Tweed on one side, and the mixed woodland on the other ringing to a variety of bird song, including great tits and chaffinches. This was a place where bird life abounded. I wondered whether the peregrines that nested in the surrounding hills ever ventured down this way on hunting forays.

A great spotted woodpecker made its presence felt with a machine-gun like rattling that resonated through the riparian woodland as it furiously drummed its bill against a hollow tree bough to advertise its presence to other woodpeckers. Then, a bold yet lilting song drifted across the air. At first, I thought it was blackbird, but no, the song was subtly different and more hesitant in its delivery.

There it went again, one melancholy phrase, followed by a pause, before moving onto the next phrase. Up high, perched on the top of a pine, I eventually spotted the source of the sweet music – a mistle thrush. Even when the wind is blowing, and every other bird has hunkered down, mistle thrushes have the indomitable spirit of spilling forth their rich songs from the tops of trees. The bird is even known as the 'storm cock' because of its penchant to sing when the weather is inclement. This mistle thrush sang for a while longer, before his wondrous melody ceased, and the tumbling background rush of the Tweed predominated once more.

On reaching the viaduct, I gazed down into the clear river below in the hope of spotting a trout, or perhaps even a grayling swimming over the shingle beds. Luck was not with me, for no trout or ladies-of-the-stream surfaced, and instead my mind drifted as if part of the river's flow.

Chapter 3

CROONING EIDERS AND
WHITE-BLUSHED BLACKTHORNS

March 2021 – Berwickshire

At the quaint fishing harbour of Burnmouth in Berwickshire, only a few kilometres from the border with England, the soft-toned calls of eider drakes rose above the gentle surge of the sea that lapped against the quayside in diminishing ripples. The call of the eider is one of the quintessential sounds of a Scottish spring down by the shore, an appreciative 'coo-or' drifting across the sea breeze as drake eiders unleash their crooning love songs out on the water. Their call is haunting and evocative, and one that stirs fond childhood memories guddling about in rock pools in search of crabs and fish.

Nestled between Eyemouth and Berwick-upon-Tweed in Northumberland, Burnmouth has for many years been one my regular haunts as it repeatedly draws one in with an irresistible pull. This is a place where the cries of herring gulls hang in the air and the sea is an ever-changing palette of colour, sometimes blue and benign, sometimes grey and threatening.

The early spring sun shone down upon the silver-speckled water of the outer basin of the harbour, where a small group of eider ducks had congregated. They were in a frisky mood, with the amorous drakes throwing back their heads in noisy admiration of the females, which bobbed up and down in amongst them.

Eider Duck (Burnmouth)

The natural drama which unfolded before my eyes was addictive. 'Coo-or, coo-or' was followed by short, white-splashed chases as the excited drakes pursued the somewhat reluctant and harassed-looking females. Whilst these calls were soft and alluring, eider courtship is often frantic, and sometimes vicious.

A few years previously, I witnessed a lone female eider in Largo Bay in Fife being hounded by a large group of drakes. She was surrounded by testosterone-fuelled black and white plumaged males, her brown head just visible in among them. The water all around her bubbled and foamed from the rapid paddling of the feet by the over-zealous drakes as they bumped and barged aggressively into her, and she soon disappeared within the midst of this boiling maelstrom. I suspect she had dived under to make good her escape. It was nature at its wildest and most extreme, and one that left me harrowed by the apparent sheer violence of intent.

Eiders are well-known for their fluffy insulating feathers and from the earliest of times eiderdown has been a valuable resource. Although synthetic alternatives or domestic goose feathers have now largely taken over, eiderdown is still much sought after as a filler for bedding and clothing. In Iceland, it is collected from the lining of nests towards the end of the breeding season without disturbing the birds.

A less-sustainable approach was adopted in Scotland in times past, with both the down and eggs removed from the nest at the same time. In the late nineteenth century, eider eggs were annually sent from Islay to Glasgow poulterers. Today, eiders, like most birds, are fully protected by law.

Cryptically feathered, the female duck relies on her mottled-brown camouflage to avoid detection and sits tightly on her eggs. In some places, eiders nest in high densities. On one occasion many years ago during a visit to Inchkeith island in the Firth of Forth I stumbled upon eider nests every few metres – the females erupted at my feet in a series of heart-stopping explosions as they took to the air. It was like treading through a minefield and I hastened a retreat to avoid further disturbance. Almost all of the ducks squirted a dollop of foul-smelling faecal matter over their eggs as they took flight. While this may have been an unfortunate consequence of spending a long time on the nest, it could also have been a last-ditch ploy to deter predators.

The eiders at Burnmouth soon settled down from their early season courting and drifted out towards the harbour entrance. Further along the outer breakwater, two fishermen were preparing boxes of fish discards to be used as bait in their lobster and crab creels. On the rocky shore opposite, small groups of oystercatchers and redshanks slumbered, heads tucked under their wings.

Down at the base of the quayside a bull grey seal surfaced accompanied by an exhalation of briny breath, his head momentarily appearing, before sliding under again. Despite this flurry of activity, the animal had previously been sleeping just under the water and had come up for air. Soon he hung motionless below the surface once more, his grey-skinned back occasionally arching out the water, revealing deep scratches and scars from a lifetime of tribulation, likely from storms at sea and battles with other seals.

Bull Grey Seal (Burnmouth Quayside)

A piercing whistle from one of the nearby creel fishermen broke the calm. It was a beckoning call and the seal awakened with a jolt. With the speed and agility of a porpoise, the seal undulated over to the side of the quay, where the fisherman tossed a gurnard towards it. The grateful seal picked the fish up in its jaws and played with it in the same manner as a dog does with a bone, tossing it into the air repeatedly. He swam further out, and paused for a while, holding the gurnard with his front flippers while he contentedly crunched through its head and bones.

It was fascinating behaviour and one which illustrated the deep intelligence of this seal in recognising the whistle as a signal for food.

With my interest aroused, I struck up a conversation with the fisherman. Despite being a male, this beast was affectionally called 'Lucille the seal', and a younger animal was also a regular visitor to the harbour to be fed.

I had witnessed seal feeding by fishermen on previous visits to Burnmouth. On one occasion a crewman leant over the stern of his boat to dangle a fish, which a seal gently plucked from his hand. With so many depressing stories about wildlife cruelty and persecution these days, it was heartening to see two potential competitors – seal and fisherman – united in friendship and respect – an uplifting moment where humanity and nature were as one.

On the way up the coast to my next destination of St Abbs, I dropped into nearby Eyemouth, where more grey seals plied the waters of the harbour. On a breakwater, a pair of turnstones pattered by on twinkling feet, probing here and there, searching for tiny morsels to feast upon. These attractive winter-visiting waders from the Arctic have short bills designed for deftly turning over pebbles and fronds of seaweed in search of invertebrates sheltering beneath. They have developed a liking for quaysides and are a common sight at Eyemouth and other east coast harbours.

Most harbours, whether large or small, are havens for marine wildlife because their protected confines offer places to shelter, especially when it is stormy. During winter in Peterhead harbour in the north east of Scotland, it is common to see good numbers of seals sheltering from gales. At Peterhead, there is the added attraction of fish being accidentally spilled overboard from fishing boats as they land to the market.

Herring Gulls (St Abbs Harbour)

St Abbs is a delightful fishing village that lies a short distance north of Eyemouth, and its rich clear waters and offshore reefs and skerries make it a magnet for sub-aqua divers. Herring gulls wheeled above the harbour, and one eagle-eyed pair had even discovered a brimming and unprotected plastic creel-bait box, from which they leisurely picked over the contents. The living here was easy, and the casual manner which the gulls inspected the fish box contents suggested they were not in the least hungry.

Herring gulls are often despised as unwelcome pests in coastal towns and villages, noisily nesting on roofs and fouling cars and pavements. In contrast, I hold herring gulls with a sneaky regard, for they are intelligent and adaptable birds.

When passing a playing field or park where herring gulls are present, it is worth stopping for a moment to observe their behaviour. If scrutinised closely, it is usually possible to see gulls engaged in the bizarre act of rapidly stamping their feet up and down, almost as if running on the spot. It has been likened by some as a gull version of *Riverdance*, but it is in reality a rather clever feeding tactic, for the vibrations caused by the rhythmic pattering of the feet mimics the vibration of raindrops, thus causing earthworms to come to the surface only to be snapped up by the hungry birds.

Such behaviour characterises the soul of the herring gull, which is hallmarked by opportunism and an ability to be at home in a variety of environments. This is a bird equally content feeding naturally on the shore or following a trawler at sea, as it is turning over the surface of an inland rubbish tip or scavenging the contents of discarded fast-food containers on the streets of Aberdeen on a Saturday night.

I wandered further around the small harbour until my eyes were drawn northwards to the nearby cliffs of St Abbs Head, a magnificent rocky and multi-indented promontory that juts out into the North Sea. Through my binoculars, I could see several fulmars on outstretched wings riding the deflected air currents close to the cliff edge.

A multitude of black dots against the cliff were brought into focus, revealing large groups of guillemots which had congregated on the broader, gently sloping rock shelves. Despite only being early March, these little black and white auks were already thinking about the breeding season ahead. A surge of excitement coursed through my veins that stirred vivid recollections of the many other seabird cliffs I know so well around Scotland.

These guillemots, which belong to the same family as puffins, were excitedly inspecting their nesting ledges, as well as engaging in courtship displays by rapidly bowing their heads up and down. It would be a couple of months before they laid their eggs, but this was all about establishing pair bonds and socialising. After a winter of oceanic wanderings across storm-tossed seas, the birds looked delighted to be back in each other's company. I knew from experience that these early season communal gatherings are erratic, and that if I returned the next day there would probably be no guillemots present. As spring progresses, however, the cliff ledges soon become permanently occupied in preparation for laying eggs.

This wild Berwickshire coast was absorbing, and it was hard to pull myself away from St Abbs, but there were other places further north that beckoned: Dunglass Burn and the adjacent shore near Cockburnspath, which forms the border divide with East Lothian. This is where I used to wild camp when a teenager, and it was wonderful to wander once more down this narrow, wooded dene towards the sea. On either side of the track, the green, shiny, broad leaves of ramsons, or wild garlic, proliferated, and in a sunny clearing I stumbled upon the pinkish blooms of red dead-nettle, one of our earliest emerging wildflowers.

The final stretch, which is part of the John Muir Link coastal path route, led me through a thick stand of sea buckthorn bushes, which I did not recall as being present in the same proliferation several decades ago. There was also a lone blackthorn, which was on the verge of flowering. I paused to look closer at the twisted, prickly branches and stems.

The prickly blackthorn is a shrub to be treated with respect and it was with great care that I examined the about-to-emerge white flowerheads. From a distance, they could easily have been mistaken as leaf buds, but a closer look revealed the whiteness of the tiny flowers that were about to burst open. In a matter of days, the bush would explode into a white-frosted splendour, which make flowering blackthorns one of the most stunning sights of spring.

The unusual thing about the blackthorn is that it flowers first, with the leaves following later. Even when the weather turns to freezing, the flowers will still blossom, with a cold spring traditionally being known as a 'blackthorn winter'.

The nineteenth-century poet, Christina Rossetti, brought into sharp focus the striking beauty of the blackthorn as it was about to blossom, or 'blow', in her poem, 'Endure Hardness':

A cold wind stirs the blackthorn
To burgeon and to blow,
Besprinkling half-green hedges
With flakes and sprays of snow.

Through coldness and through keenness,
Dear hearts, take comfort so:
Somewhere or other doubtless
These make the blackthorn blow.

The blackthorn's white blossom is alluring for early emerging bumblebees and other insects, and once the leaves are set, they are a principal food for many different types of moth larvae. The blackthorn is important to wildlife in other ways. The impenetrable tangle of twigs and thorns makes the shrub a great favourite of birds as a safe place to build their nests. Birds are also attracted by the many caterpillars found upon their leaves.

The blackthorn is best known for its bitter-tasting fruits that we know familiarly as sloes, which are used for making wine and jams and for flavouring gin. Sloes are high in Vitamin C and have been foraged since the earliest of times. Sloe stones have even been found in the refuse remains of Neolithic settlements.

The sea was a short distance away. Soon, I was upon the rocky beach, with the distant sloping spur of Fast Castle Head lying to the south, and the nearby incongruous grey block of Torness nuclear power station dominating the north. The foreshore here was boulder strewn and beyond that lay a broad seaweed-covered, tidal rock shelf. Many moons ago, I snorkelled in a deep gully that cuts into this shelf, a wonderful kelp-forested underwater paradise where ballan wrasse, short-spined sea scorpion fish, and crimson-coloured beadlet anemones abounded.

It didn't take me long to find this deep cleft from memories past, but the wind had picked up, and the turbulent sea surged back and forwards with a menacing intensity, stirring sediment and making it impossible to peer down into its dark watery depths.

On my way back across the seaweed encrusted rocks, a small group of wigeon dabbled nearby in a series of pools where the Dunglass Burn spilled out onto the shore. These ducks were foraging upon eel grass, one of their favourite winter staples.

The drakes in this little flock were a picture of pastel softness, with yellowish fore-partings on burnt-sienna heads, subtle lilac breasts and shimmering, silvery bodies. Everything about the wigeon is gentle and benign. It is a bird that oozes warmth.

It was difficult to get my head around the fact that some of these fragile-looking ducks could have migrated several thousand miles to spend the winter in this little corner of south-east Scotland. Small numbers of wigeon do breed in Scotland, but most of those found on our winter lochs and shores are visitors from Iceland, Scandinavia and Russia. Some even hail from as far afield as central Siberia and one can only imagine the dangers faced during such daunting migrations.

Safe stopover points are crucial during these mammoth journeys, which is why nature conservation needs to be an international affair. Many migrating wigeon spend time on the Pripyat river floodplain in southern Belarus on their way to Western Europe and the protection of such areas is as crucial to their protection as the conservation of our own wetlands and coasts. There are no boundaries in nature, for they are imaginary and arbitrary lines drawn by humanity, which serve no meaningful purpose nor use.

By chance, several weeks after my visit to this stretch of coast, Jack Wootton, a freshwater ecologist with the Forth Rivers Trust, invited me for an electro-fishing session on the Dunglass Burn. Jack's interest is the eel, which he is studying through the 'Forgotten Fish Project' at the Forth Rivers Trust. The work includes assessing the status of the eels in the Forth catchment area and identifying and implementing measures that will improve their survival. This is especially important, given that eel numbers have plummeted in recent decades for reasons that include climate change, pollution, overfishing and barriers, such as weirs, impeding access to rivers.

Eels play a fundamental role in our freshwater ecosystems. They are a vital source of food for otters, herons and other fish-eating water creatures, and when eels grow larger, they themselves become predators of fish and invertebrates.

Eels are little slivers of mystery that spawn in the far away Sargasso Sea, north east of the Greater Antilles. The Sargasso Sea has no land boundary and is located entirely within the Atlantic Ocean. It is characterised by free-floating sargassum, a common seaweed found there. In what must rank as one of the most incredible of biological feats, the tiny glass-like larvae gradually drift back the 6,000 km journey to Europe on the North Atlantic Drift before ascending Scotland's rivers, where they turn into elvers and over time grow into larger eels. After many years in a river or estuary, they make the return journey via the Azores to spawn.

As well as using traps, electro-fishing is a specialist technique that researchers can use to assess eel populations. There is a weir on the lower part of Dunglass Burn near the sea, and on our visit, Jack was keen to electro-fish above and below the obstruction to make comparisons of the fish present. Accompanied by Scot Muir of the Trust, we waded slowly upstream, with Jack sweeping an anode into the water ahead of him. Scot was right behind to quickly lift into his net any fish temporarily immobilised by the electrical current, which are placed into a bucket of water for later examination and recording, before being released back unharmed into the burn.

The gorge here, below the imposing bridges that carry the A1 dual carriageway and the main east coast railway line, was like a different world: a dark and impenetrable place where dampness hung heavy in the air and shade and moisture-loving liverworts abounded. A dipper whirred upstream on fast beating wings and a grey wagtail flashed overhead.

During the electro-fishing, nothing was caught above the weir, whilst below it, several small trout swept up into the net. An eel tantalisingly appeared for a brief moment in the swirl of surface water, but managed to escape. The difference in the catches above and below the weir told its own compelling story of how this man-made structure from the past was impacting upon fish and their ability to move within the burn. For the eels, it effectively meant there was only 300m of burn they could utilise between the sea and the weir.

To overcome this impediment, a few weeks later, Jack and Scot completed the installation of a simple, robust fish pass that connected into a lade adjacent to the weir, enabling eels and trout to move freely up and down the water course, thus opening up vital new habitat. By offering this helping hand, the eels of the Dunglass Burn had been given a fighting chance for survival.

Chapter 4

SPRING FLOWERS AND DANCING GREBES

April 2021 – Ayr Gorge Woodlands and Lochwinnoch

Dawn is compelling and often a time of great stillness, when hardly a riffle of wind brushes the high treetops, and where only the tumble of river or burn, and the songs of stirring birds seeps upon the consciousness. I had only just arrived at Ayr Gorge Woodlands, a few miles from Mauchline in East Ayrshire, yet had become instantly smitten by its warm, welcoming hold. The sweet aroma of garlic filled the dawn air, a pleasing and redolent odour, drawn from the heart of the soil. The garlicky smell came and went, sometimes intense, yet intermittently weakening, becoming more subtle and lightly perfumed.

This natural fragrance emanated from a green-glossed covering of ramsons, or wild garlic as they are often known, that clung to a bankside by the River Ayr. Now a Scottish Wildlife Trust reserve, Ayr Gorge Woodlands is an imposing place of towering oaks and ashes, and red sandstone cliffs that have been sculpted by glacial meltwater some 10,000 years ago. It is one of the most important woodlands in Ayrshire for invertebrates, plants, fungi and bats.

Robert Burns once walked here, and he later composed a poem about the gorge, along with 'Highland Mary', a local lass he courted:

> *That sacred hour can I forget,*
> *Can I forget the hallow'd grove,*
> *Where by the winding Ayr, we met,*
> *To live one day of parting love!*
>
> ('To Mary in Heaven', 1789)

The ramsons were not quite in flower, their white blousy blooms still tantalisingly held within their green sepals, yet heavy with intent to burst into their full glory. The plant is sometimes known as 'stinking nanny',

Ramsons

which is a comparison I find inappropriate, as their fragrance is soothing and balm-like.

Ramsons thrive in shady woods, especially by rivers and burns, and other damp margins. In Continental Europe, brown bears adore eating ramson bulbs, which is reflected in their scientific name, *Allium ursinum*, that is derived from the Latin *ursus*, meaning bear. This gives rise to two of its other common names, bear's leek and bear garlic. The elongated, flat leaves are much sought after for those with a culinary disposition, and provide an aromatic garlic flavouring to salads, tasting best before the flowers appear, when they are at their most tender and verdant. Ramsons were once revered by herbalists and used to treat digestive problems, rheumatism and asthma.

Great woodrush was similarly abundant on the ground by my feet. It is one of our more understated spring flowers, with its loose clusters of tiny chestnut brown blooms and dense tussocks of narrow arching leaves, failing to shine in the way other woodland plants do. I like underdogs, so took time to examine their flowers more closely. They are miniscule but have a complexity of form that deserves greater appreciation.

Moving on, my eyes were continually drawn to the ground, and the path, which is part of the River Ayr walking route, unfolded a richness of other emerging plants, including creeping tendrils of honeysuckle draped over stunted hazel trees.

Although not yet in flower, the distinctive clover-like leaves of wood sorrel were beginning to gain prominence in some parts of the gorge. Wood sorrel often prospers on moss-covered tree stumps and fallen trunks, and like woodrush, exhibits a muted elegance that is easy to miss. Once in bloom, it is worth scrutinising this flower closely, for what from a distance appear as completely white petals are in fact gently scribbled with lilac.

Great Woodrush

By the base of a beech tree, a clump of primroses shimmered. The primrose is perhaps the ultimate spring beauty and one of the first to flower. The crinkled oval green leaves are visible for a month or so before almost miraculously the pastel yellow flowers suddenly appear. The softness of the yellow is like a hallucination and there are few more stirring sights than a bank of primroses bathed in the sunlight of a dew-filled spring morning. Its common name is derived from *prima rosa* – meaning first rose – and is a reference to its early flowering (although the plant is not a rose).

I sat for a while on a moss-covered tumbled tree trunk, soaking up the crisp morning air and listening to a distant song thrush. On the river, a small group of courting mallards chased each other in a frenzy of flapping wings before settling down once more.

Sitting motionless with hardly a flicker of a muscle, until you blend seamlessly into the landscape, is such a productive way for seeking out wildlife. Nature is not just about the birds and other creatures that move. It is also about the plants and the trees, and the fungi, lichens and mosses. By remaining in one place for a period and observing the immediate environment, so much appears that might otherwise be overlooked. Here, in this little microcosm of Ayrshire, small ferns clung to the low boughs of trees, a dipper whizzed upriver, and a queen buff-tailed bumblebee buzzed and hovered over the ground, looking for a hole or crevice to settle down and form a new colony. Every autumn, the workers, drones and old queens die off as the cold weather takes its grip leaving behind just young, fertilised queens, who hibernate, before emerging in spring to start the cycle of life once more.

A fluttering caught the corner of my eye. It was a treecreeper, a wee mouse of a bird that had appeared from nowhere and was rapidly crawling up the

Treecreeper (Ayr Gorge)

narrow trunk of a low tree. On reaching the top, it flitted down to the base of the next tree and then spiralled jerkily up that one too. In some ways, it behaves a bit like a woodpecker, but rather than hammering at a trunk to dig out invertebrates, the treecreeper has a lighter touch, using its long curved slender bill to nimbly pick out tiny creatures from crevices in the bark. Precision is everything, and I recall once seeing a treecreeper extract a diminutive spider from a hairline crack in an apple tree, using its bill like a pair of tweezers and deftly removing it with all the sureness of a surgeon.

The treecreeper undulated across to another tree before it was soon gone from view. The air was quiet once more, save for the song thrush, which continued its haunting melody.

I rose to my feet and continued further downstream along the River Ayr until reaching Peden's Cove. Steps were cut into the sandstone cliff here in the seventeenth century to enable the Covenanter, Alexander Peden, to preach to his congregation on the other side of the river. Peden was legendary for his premonitions and was often referred to as Prophet Peden.

During the return journey to my starting point at the hamlet of Failford, a pair of roe deer which had ventured down to the riverside, bounded away in long, leaping strides, their white rumps flashing like beacons. The dark brown, peaty waters of the River Ayr looked strangely seductive, revealing in places broad underwater rock shelves, where salmon must shelter when they run upriver.

Peden's Cove (Ayr Gorge, Ayrshire)

Any type of water body, whether river, loch or pond, has an addictive nature, which proved the lure that drew me later that morning to Lochwinnoch in Renfrewshire. Rather than being a loch, Lochwinnoch is the name of the small town by the River Calder, which lies adjacent to Castle Semple Loch and Barr Loch, which are separated from each other by a narrow strip of land. The River Calder fills Castle Semple Loch and then drains out as the Black Cart Water, which flows into the River Clyde.

The sky had clouded over and a gentle breeze brushed the air. From the RSPB visitor centre near Lochwinnoch, a path led down to the shore edge at Castle Semple Loch. It had suddenly turned cold, and I pulled up my jacket collar and hunkered down for protection. In among a tangle of willows, a mute swan warmed her nest in preparation for egg laying, and repeatedly swayed her long neck back and forwards as she collected reeds and other vegetation to add to the edges of her nesting platform.

The loch itself held an abundant variety of waterfowl but it was a pair of great crested grebes which quickly became the star attraction. Grebes are among my favourite water birds and I think this adoration stems from discovering a couple of rare Slavonian grebes on a small lochan in Moray in the mid-1980s. I recall vividly the astounding plumage of these birds, with their black cheeks offset by golden ear tufts and russet body providing a wonderful contrast against the silvery glass-like sheen of the lochan. It is a stunning bird, but despite its colour and vibrancy, grebes often go unnoticed, having the capacity to blend and merge into their watery environment.

Great Crested Grebe (Castle Semple Loch)

The two great crested grebes out on Castle Semple Loch brought such memories flooding back. As I observed them through my binoculars, they began to court one another, swimming apart and repeatedly rushing back to face up to one another, shaking their chestnut-frilled heads from side-to-side. Courtship often involves the collection of pondweeds in their sharp bills, which is then shown off to one another like some prize trophy. It is a bird dance that outshines all others, such is the synchronisation and variety of movement.

In Victorian times, the colourful plumage of the great crested grebe was much prized for fashionable clothing – in particular, the satin breast or 'grebe fur'. The feathers were also sought after by anglers for fly-tying. All this, combined with the activities of egg collectors, resulted in persecution on such a scale that the British population was almost totally decimated. However, this was one cloud that had a silver lining as the plight of the great crested grebe led directly to the founding of the RSPB in 1889 to counter the trade in plumes for women's hats, which was one of the key landmarks in the historical development of the international conservation movement.

Thankfully, the great crested grebe population has now recovered, although it is still a scarce nester in Scotland because of its dependence on shallow, fertile lowland lochs and reservoirs, combined with at least some patches of reeds or other marginal waterside growth for nesting.

The courting grebes on Castle Semple Loch were some distance away and it was uncomfortable on the eyes to watch them for any length of time through my binoculars. The breeze had suddenly eased, so I put the eyepieces away and savoured instead the calming influences of the loch. A small flight of sand martins swooped low over the water. They had just arrived from Africa and were a heart-warming signal that spring and the season of renewal was now gathering pace. The magic of the loch had taken grip and my thoughts turned once more to previous encounters with grebes, sparking an inner desire to delve deeper into their fascinating lives.

Chapter 5

UNDERGROUND LIVING WATER VOLES AND SEVEN LOCHS

April 2021 – East End of Glasgow

The ground beneath our feet was soft, yielding and pock-marked with little burrows. There, on a small patch of grassland in the east end of Glasgow, surrounded by houses and with the constant hum of the M8 motorway nearby, we stood upon something extraordinary.

The burrows, which were not immediately obvious to the eye, belonged to water voles, yet there was no ditch, pond nor burn nearby. In an anomaly of nature, water voles in the east end of Glasgow have shunned water and instead prosper in grasslands, living much of their lives in underground burrows. This behaviour is not uncommon among water voles in Continental Europe but is rarely recorded in Britain.

Water Vole (Cranhill Park, Glasgow)

Water vole burrows in grassland are not immediately obvious to the eye but I was fortunate to be accompanied by Cath Scott, Natural Environment Officer for Glasgow City Council, who was taking me on a tour of some of their sites, of which there are many in this part of Glasgow and North Lanarkshire. Our first stop was Avenue End Primary School where voles were inhabiting a nearby grassy bank. The school children adore the voles, which are often the subject of projects.

Underground living (fossorial) water voles were first discovered in Glasgow's east end in 2008. They are the same species as wetland dwelling water voles but make their home in parks, road verges, vacant land, gardens and wherever else they find long grass and can burrow. According to Cath, their origin is a mystery.

> They could have always been living an underground lifestyle in this area but only came to our attention as surveys were extended to include grassland habitat... Alternatively, this may be a new phenomenon and they have adapted to living in grasslands when water courses were lost during building development in the east end, including the construction of the nearby M8 motorway in the 1950s.

Certainly, there are several wetland sites in proximity to the east end where aquatic living water voles exist. Interestingly, where recent construction work in the area has created SUDS (Sustainable Urban Drainage Systems) pools, these are sometimes occupied by water voles, suggesting the creatures are adaptable to either habitat, and can mix and match.

The site where grassland water voles were first found in Glasgow was our next destination, and as we gazed in fascination down upon the multitude of burrows in the grass, it was hard to imagine that water voles have experienced catastrophic decline in recent decades, due to habitat loss, and most notably, predation by American mink. In stark contrast, here in Glasgow's east end, water voles are thriving, and their fossorial habits bring a distinct advantage in that mink are generally tied to water, thus predation is not a major issue.

I crouched down to examine one of the burrows. The entrance was small at about 8cm in diameter. The surprising aspect was that there were so many tunnels in proximity to one another. The burrows of aquatic water voles, which are set in a linear fashion along riverbanks, are fewer and further between. Research led by the University of Glasgow has shown that voles do better on grassland sites than by water. Nearby Cranhill Park, for example, has the highest density of water voles in the east end – 156 animals per hectare, which is also believed to be the highest density in the UK. It would appear that despite water voles being territorial and requiring their own living space, grasslands manage to support much higher concentrations than water living populations.

The combination of their unusual grassland dwelling behaviour and high numbers means that Glasgow's water voles are now recognised as nationally significant and may be crucial for the future conservation of water voles in the UK. According to Cath:

> *This large population of water voles could act as a reservoir for reintroduction schemes in other parts of the country where the animals have become extinct or much diminished, although care needs to be taken to ensure they have the same genetic integrity as the original populations, and we also need to make sure the east end of Glasgow population is safe first.*

During winter, the voles spend most of their time in their underground tunnels and chambers, feeding on food stores of vegetation and nibbling plant roots from below. The impact of this root chewing was easily discerned, with some areas of grass looking brown and wilted. Once spring arrives, the voles become increasingly active and spend more time on the surface foraging. Although the voles do not have to worry about mink, they do face other dangers, included being dug out by domestic dogs; and whenever they venture above ground being predated upon by cats, foxes, buzzards and grey herons. There is the additional hazard of the voles being mistaken by local people as brown rats, with the resultant pest control measures having the potential to wreak havoc.

The Glasgow voles were most intriguing and it was hard to draw myself away from the grassy area where they proliferated. Once my eyes had become tuned into the presence of the voles, their signs became distinctive. One noticeable feature was the subtle undulating nature of the ground, caused by their digging activities. Such earthworks are not as substantial as molehills, forming instead little mounds and ridges.

The grassland we were standing upon is being studied by Cath and others as part of a project to assess the impact of grass mowing on the vole population. It is desirable to keep a core area of long grass for the water voles but also to carry out low-intensity traditional meadow management in some areas to improve the botanical diversity for other wildlife priorities such as insect pollinators. Allowing access for local residents to enjoy their local greenspace is also a priority, so informal path routes are mown and high-profile areas have been enhanced by wildflower planting and sowing.

Water voles are legally protected, and this site is a NatureScot trial to determine whether grassland mowing has any impact on numbers, and to find the optimum frequency of mowing and level of cut. As Cath explained:

> There are some very high population densities of voles in this area. One of our key aims is to ensure there is connectivity between the various grasslands in the east end which hold water voles to ensure the overall population can prosper. These populations are vulnerable to local extinction through habitat loss and fragmentation because of development. This means liaising with building companies when development is happening to ensure vole habitat is retained. Sometimes voles are moved to other nearby areas to save populations affected by house building, and we work closely with developers to provide habitat and minimise impact.

A short while later, we arrived at the massive Glasgow Fort shopping centre, which must rank as one of Scotland's most unusual wildlife sanctuaries. On its southern flank, bordering the M8, is a large green wall – a supporting buttress that is grassed over on its vertical surface, creating in effect, a grass cliff. As we peered over a fence from the top of this grass precipice down upon the motorway, I was astonished to learn that water voles live in burrows within its steep confines. The noise from the traffic on the M8 was intense, yet the voles are not in the least bothered by the disturbance. They have adapted with ease to their high-rise tenement style living, safe from predators within this formidable fortress. I imagine the voles gain additional benefit from the south facing aspect of the grass wall, providing welcome warmth from the sun during winter.

Fossorial water vole colonies are found along other parts of the M8 in the east end of Glasgow and near the border with North Lanarkshire, which raises the intriguing possibility that they have the potential to spread all the way to Edinburgh – or perhaps they have already done so; no survey work has been carried out to see if this is the case.

Glasgow's east end has other nature attractions, and on that same day, I spent time at Hogganfield Park Local Nature Reserve. The centrepiece is Hogganfield Loch, a large shallow water body, which is one of a series of kettle ponds in the area formed during the last Ice Age. A fresh, invigorating breeze blew across the water, and a variety of waterfowl abounded, included mute swans, goosanders and tufted ducks. A family of whooper swans are regular visitors each winter. They have become quite tame, paddling close inshore to be fed. Cath told me that ringing studies have shown that these whoopers nest on a lake by Reykjavik in Iceland, and thus have become habituated to people on both their summer and wintering grounds.

Tufted ducks on Hogganfield Loch were also approachable. They are such comical ducks with the wind-swept tufty streamers on the napes of the drakes looking like punk-style haircuts. Every so often, they roll-dived under the water in search of molluscs and other invertebrates.

Hogganfield Park is the western gateway to the Seven Lochs Wetland Park, an ambitious initiative that has brought together 20km² of lochs, parks, nature reserves and woodlands between Glasgow and Coatbridge, as a place for people to enjoy, and which celebrates both nature and heritage. I was most taken by Cath's enthusiasm for this network of lochs and wetlands, so the following day I visited Bishop Loch, which is part of the wetland park. The sun shone with brilliant intensity and out on the water floated a pair of goldeneyes. They are winter visiting ducks, which are skittish in habit, often taking to the air on whistling wings at the first hint of danger, but this pair was relaxed, mirroring the calm waters of the loch.

On the rare occasions when one is fortunate enough to be able to examine a drake goldeneye from a close distance, the vibrant yellow eyes shine out like glowing orbs. Goldeneye is certainly a most appropriate name, with those gleaming eyes having a burning intensity that lingers long in the mind. Drake pochards, another type of duck frequently found in Scotland, have similarly striking eyes, although theirs are deep scarlet rather than piercing yellow.

Goldeneye (Bishop Loch)

All this got me wondering – why such distinctive eyes? It appears there is no definitive answer, but there are several theories, including that vibrancy of the eye-colour acts as an indicator of the maturity of a bird and thus its suitability as a potential mate. With such ocular thoughts buzzing through my head, I made my way further around Bishop Loch to a vast reedbed, the largest area of common reeds (phragmites) in Glasgow.

A male reed bunting perched on top of one of the swaying reeds, his distinctive black head and white collar catching the sun. I suspected there would be more about, so I swept my binoculars back along the reeds and spotted two others, both of whom were females. Although male reed buntings are striking, they are feeble spring songsters, their tune consisting of a few rather weak notes.

I retraced my steps and then walked for a further 20 minutes in the other direction towards Commonhead Moss Local Nature Reserve, a raised bog and one of our most

Reed Bunting

important and threatened habitats. In the lowlands of Scotland, many raised bogs have been damaged and destroyed by peat extraction, drainage for agriculture and, more recently, forestry. Raised bogs provide home for a variety of unique plants, animals and insects, and can also help alleviate flooding and store carbon.

Raised bogs first developed many thousands of years ago in depressions occupied by shallow lakes, usually left behind by retreating glaciers. Over the period that followed, with the rate of accumulation of damp vegetation debris exceeding the rate of decay, the continued build-up of peat elevated the bog surface above groundwater levels to form a gently raised curving dome, a vast sponge that holds sphagnum and other mosses and damp-loving plants. Commonhead Moss, which is 25 hectares in area, has its own special biodiversity and is home to rare species such as bog rosemary and green hairstreak butterfly.

The temptation to visit another one of the seven lochs in the area was impossible to resist, and a short car journey took me to Frankfield Loch by the town of Stepps on the north eastern outskirts of Glasgow. This is an attractive loch edged by a boggy margin thick with willow carr. While there, a dabchick repeatedly dived in the shallows, searching for small fish to feed upon, until it disappeared in among the dark, thick tangle of branches.

On the far side of the loch lay a stretch of grassland where in among the tussocks was a scattering of burrows – water voles! The signs of these enchanting little rodents kept on popping up and it was reassuring to know that their special adaptation to grassland living has provided a crucial lifeline in their battle with the American mink. Glasgow's east end, and the surrounding area of North Lanarkshire, is home to one of Scotland's most remarkable natural phenomena – a wonderful reminder of nature's perennial ability to innovate and adapt.

_____

Chapter 6

FOXES AND A SUNBATHING FISH

April 2021 – North Edinburgh and Wardie Bay

The soft, resonant warbling from the tree above quickly gained in pitch and intensity. My eyes glanced upwards, and the glimmering of a robin redbreast shone from a branch, its fragile body perfect in form, its song so melodic it could have been spirited from the heavens. For an eight-year-old boy, this was an experience like no other previously encountered; an inspirational moment that has remained indelibly embedded upon my mind.

It is a frozen-in-time recollection so sharp in the memory it could have been yesterday, and then, some 50 years later, I was sitting in the exact same spot below a large sycamore at the top of an old railway embankment in the north of Edinburgh. The tree has changed markedly over the intervening period with its canopy much broader in reach, and under its creeping shade, the ground had become bare, whereas before rosebay willowherb and thick tangles of brambles enriched the steep cutting.

Back then, this robin encounter was pivotal because it was the final catalyst that sparked my love for nature and appreciation of its infinite diversity. It was an evolutionary process, and there had been several other wild encounters prior to then, which had initially set the ball rolling, each one gathering in momentum to form a greater whole.

The first memory was as a toddler when, by chance, I discovered a blackbird's nest in the garden. Cradled within a low fork, the nest held four baby blackbirds, their startling bright orange mouths gaping as they desperately begged for food. These bright bug-eyed chicks held me in trance-like wonderment, my young brain absorbing the scene with the speed of a dry sponge, yet not understanding what I was seeing.

A few years later, when at primary school, it was the unlikely medium of the once-a-week music class that further developed my nature addiction. Music at that time was of no great interest to me, but a small, attractive long-tailed bird that strutted along the hard surface of the school playground outside the classroom window most certainly was. During each music lesson, as the teacher plonked the piano keys with gusto and rallied us to sing, my lips would silently mouth the song while my eyes were continually drawn to the window. I always endeavoured to sit by this vantage point, and more times than not, especially after rain when the playground was pockmarked with shallow puddles, this little black and white beauty appeared. It wagged its tail in fevered fashion, dashing this way and that, snapping up little flies that swirled in the air.

This bird was different in shape and form from other garden birds I knew. Curiosity aroused, the bird's identity, a pied wagtail, was soon revealed in the school library's copy of the *Observer's Book of Birds* (1952). On thumbing the pages, a multitude of other birds left me in awe, many of which I had never imagined could possibly exist such was their diversity in shape and colour. Long-billed curlews, impressive falcons and miniscule goldcrests, it was a cornucopia of marvellous life. The *Observer's* companion guide on mammals, which was also in the school library, held me in similar captivation.

As fortune would have it, when my family moved to north Edinburgh, the network of railway lines and their associated embankments, along with Warriston Cemetery and the nearby Water of Leith proved an unanticipated bonus, for these were true wild green spaces brimming with wildlife, including that singing robin so clearly imprinted upon my consciousness. My parents were wonderfully relaxed whenever I ventured outdoors, for which I am eternally grateful, as on my doorstep was an Aladdin's Cave of natural richness to roam and explore at will.

With so many memories it was wonderful to return all these years later. I rose from my seat under the sycamore and ventured along the top of the embankment to an area where there was once a small grassy clearing set against a stone wall. It was here I glimpsed my first ever fox, sunning itself early one summer morning. By this early stage of life, I had become well and truly hooked, and over the years that followed spent many evenings precariously perched in trees or on the tops of walls watching Edinburgh's railway foxes. The exact reason for my fascination is hard to pinpoint, but I think it stemmed from the intrigue that a wild animal the size of a small dog could thrive in our cities.

Later, as part of my zoology degree at the University of Aberdeen,

Edinburgh's foxes came under my scientific study. Urban and country foxes are as different as chalk and cheese. One is a shy and elusive beast, seldom seen and often persecuted. The other a much bolder animal altogether, going about its daily business under our very noses, padding along our pavements, sleeping under our garden sheds, and dining-out on the remnants of discarded fast-food takeaways.

Urban foxes thrive because cities such as Edinburgh and Glasgow are not just concrete jungles, but rather an intricate patchwork of green wildness, including leafy gardens and small woods, railway embankments, parks and cemeteries, all of which serve to make an ideal foraging ground for foxes. As far as the fox is concerned, there is nothing better than a well-tended lawn on a warm, damp night for providing a veritable feast of wriggling worms.

There, in the heart of Edinburgh, the place where I was standing, lay a wildlife habitat as rich as anywhere else in Scotland I could imagine.

Urban Fox (Disused Railway Line, Edinburgh)

These railway embankments are the equivalent of sunny open glades in woods, with a rich flora that attracts bees, butterflies and other insect pollinators. The abundant brambles and nettle beds form safe refuges for blackbirds, thrushes and warblers to nest. The proliferation of lawns is perfect for birds to forage for worms, snails and other invertebrates, whilst flowerbeds and ornamental bushes provide additional nectar for insects in spring and summer, as well as life-sustaining berries in autumn. Garden bird feeders and nest boxes provide an additional helping hand, and the surrounding built environs deliver shelter from wind and cold, creating its own urban micro-climate.

A further benefit of railway embankments, both used and disused, and those that have been turned into walkways and cycleways, is that they provide continuous connecting corridors of wildness radiating from the centre of the city and out into the countryside beyond. This is important, because connectivity between wild areas in our landscape is often lost or much diminished – they are arteries which enable wildlife to move between different areas, ensuring diversity and resilience.

I clambered down from the grassy patch where I had witnessed my first fox all those years ago and onto where the railway track previously was, and which is now a tarmacked walkway. I wondered whether any of the fox dens from my younger days were still present. When I first ventured here, this was a quiet and peaceful place, although one had to be wary of roaming teenage gangs keen to pick a fight with a lone individual. Now, it was bustling, the interlinking network of routes thronged with dog walkers, joggers and cyclists. The inherent wildness that had beguiled me all those years ago, however, still seeped out from every pore, and I soon came under its spell once more.

A chiffchaff, newly arrived from its African wintering grounds, sang its simple two-syllable tune, and a female blackbird busily turned over soil by the track edge. The yellow-spangled flowers of lesser celandines glistened on the ground and shiny green leaves were emerging on trees. The plants and trees seemed to be ahead of themselves compared to the countryside nearby, probably because of the sheltered aspect of the surrounding built environment.

While there had been changes, I still recognised many of my old haunts: the high promontory by the railway track where I used to watch foxes at dusk, and a crevice in a wall by the trackside where great tits once nested. A familiar musty whiff filled the air – the smell of a fox! I took a turn along another walkway and then veered into a thick stand of vegetation towards where one of my favourite fox dens used to lie. At the time, this den was burrowed into a low bank which lay beside an area of open, grassy ground. Now, the area is totally overgrown with sycamore and luxuriant, tangled ivy.

It was difficult to get my bearings, but nonetheless I crashed through the thick twist of prickly brambles and dog rose to where I thought the den should be. Another waft of fox scent drifted across the air, even stronger and more pungent than before. On the ground, flies buzzed by the remains of a dead wood pigeon, which had probably been predated upon by a fox. I was getting close. Then, the foxhole loomed from the bankside, larger than before and with the distinctive pungent aroma that told me a vixen was below, perhaps already with new-born cubs. This den was still active, and as such, had been in regular use for at least half-a-century beforehand, potentially rearing almost 200 cubs over the period. It was an emotional discovery and memories flooded back of the numerous times that I had perched in a hawthorn above this den to watch the cubs at play, tumbling and rolling in their youthful innocence.

One of the most influential wildlife books from my youth was David Stephen's *A Guide to Watching Wildlife* (1963). From it, I had learnt that to successfully watch foxes and badgers, it was best to get above the ground in a tree or other high vantage point, so that one's smell would not be detected by their keen noses. The hawthorn above this den was an uncomfortable place to perch, so I had nailed a wooden plank to one of the branches to provide a seat. It was a ploy I used to similar good effect when watching badgers in the nearby Corstorphine Woods.

One popular myth about urban foxes is that they kill cats. While this may occasionally be true, in the numerous encounters I have witnessed between the two, more times than not the fox backs down, or is even forced to flee from the tetchy feline, which is a formidable foe once its hackles have been raised. Other pets, however, may occasionally get taken. I once found the remains of a tortoise outside a fox den in Edinburgh and guinea pigs and pet rabbits also sometimes meet a similar fate. As David Stephen remarked, foxes do not carry keys and can only gain access to an outdoors chicken run, guinea pig or rabbit hutch if the owner has not properly secured it.

Although wary, the urban fox is amazingly indifferent to humans. I have noticed a big difference in this level of tolerance compared to when I first started to watch urban foxes in the 1970s. They were still quite shy then but now it is not uncommon in the evenings to watch them trot along the pavements of our towns and cities with carefree nonchalance.

This relaxed view of life also extends to where they site their dens, for when I returned to the main walkway after having just viewed the 50-year-old den, it was easy to spot several more dens along various stretches of the embankments, plain for all the world to see.

The fox, whether urban or country, is one of the animal success stories of modern times. It is everywhere, in our towns, fields, woods and mountains. Some people do not like the animal, whether it be a sheep farmer convinced that their lambs are being preyed upon, or a householder who has had their pristine lawn dug up by an inquisitive cub. But perhaps we also see a little bit of the intelligent fox in us, hence the long-held admiration many people hold for one of Scotland's most remarkable wild animals.

Earlier that same day I revisited one of my other favoured haunts from the past, nearby Wardie Bay, where at low tide, I once enthusiastically turned over rocks in search of fish and crabs. This bay in the Firth of Forth is artificial in form, having been created by the outer breakwaters of Granton Harbour to the west, and Newhaven and Leith Docks on the other side. For a youngster, this provided an alluring and compelling contrast between the terrestrial wildlife found on the railway embankments and the marine creatures of the bay.

Flipping rocks over at low tide several decades ago was an extreme hygiene hazard, which in childhood ignorance I was totally oblivious to, for there was a sewage outfall pipe in the bay, and the shore spilled with raw human waste. Peculiarly, at the time, the outfalls at Edinburgh, most notably at Seafield between Leith and Portobello, were a major attraction to sea ducks – such as eiders, scaup and scoters – in the winter which congregated in huge offshore rafts to feed upon the grain from distillery and brewery waste, as well as on some types of marine invertebrate life that prospered on the raw sewage.

Thankfully, the Firth of Forth has now been largely cleaned up and pumping raw sewage into the water is consigned to the past. With the large winter congregations of sea ducks long gone, I was keen to find if the cleaner water had changed the dynamic of the inshore fish and other marine life. Previously, I had discovered large numbers of eelpouts and butterfish when searching the intertidal pools, and mussels were abundant. The eelpout, or viviparous blenny as it is also known, is a long-bodied fish, with a small head and slimy skin. The butterfish is similarly elongated, with a laterally compressed body, and is even more slimy than the eelpout, slithering through fingers with the ease of a wedge of butter.

Having chosen a morning with a low spring tide, I ventured down to a small sandy beach by the edge of the east breakwater at Granton, and then worked eastwards towards Newhaven Harbour, turning over rocks all the while in search of creatures. The sky was overcast, yet there was a spring warmth to the air, and out on the water small groups of eiders and herring gulls bobbed, along with a cormorant, which continually roll-dived in search of fish.

Soon, I was in intertidal heaven for under each rock was a plethora of life, much more than from the past, although there were noticeably fewer mussels than before; perhaps they were one of the creatures that had benefited from past pollution. Every rock turned proved a treasure trove: starfish-like brittle stars with their thin, fragile arms abounded, as did purple-hued ragworms and diminutive hairy crabs. From recollection, these creatures were not present when the shore was polluted. Many of the rocks here are flat, and slab-like, which offers ample shelter for creatures to hide. Butterfish were also abundant, although only one eelpout was revealed, which shot away into deeper water before I could catch it.

From under another small slab wriggled a dark-greenish fish, about 10cm long, called a shanny, its body glistening under the water. I scooped it out with cupped hands. The feisty fish bit with its jaws into a soft, fleshy fold of my forefinger, hanging on grimly until I gently lowered it back into the pool where it made good its escape.

Shanny (Wardie Bay)

Shannies are interesting because they are often found basking in the sunshine by rockpool margins. A sunbathing fish, surely not? But yes, that is exactly what shannies often do, soaking up the sun's rays in water no more than a few millimetres deep, presumably to warm up and save energy. There must be risks attached by exposing themselves. Shannies are, however, wary and well camouflaged, and if one approaches too close, they will invariably quickly dash away to safety.

The shanny can happily survive for several hours out of water, and if unable to find a suitable pool when the tide recedes, will secrete itself under wet seaweed or in a rocky crevice. It can slither across rocks from one rockpool to another, hence why it is sometimes known as the sea frog.

By the water's edge, a pair of turnstones dashed this way and that, so tame that I was able to approach within a few metres of them. I scanned the sea with my binoculars, and in among the eiders swam a pair of long-tailed ducks. They are exquisite, the drake so perfectly proportioned with his soft rounded head and long spiky tail. Long-tailed ducks mainly breed on the Arctic tundra and come to our coasts to spend the winter.

Turnstones (Wardie Bay)

My attention focused back once more on searching the mud and rocks of the intertidal pools. Wardie Bay is Edinburgh's most important site for fossils, the flat-lying black mudstone there holding many types of fossil, which have been collected and studied since the 1820s. These fossils are well preserved in ironstone nodules that are harder than mudstone and are left behind when the mudstone erodes away. During the 1970s, the famous amateur palaeontologist, Stan Wood, took an interest in the site and discovered 15 different types of fossilised fish. Apparently, he boiled all the rocks he collected to sterilise them from the sewage pollutants, a hygiene precaution that never occurred to my youthful mind at the time. Today, this is a Site of Special Scientific Interest, and the hammering of rocks in search of fossils is not allowed without permission.

As my pool search was nearing an end, the familiar shape of a mermaid's purse caught my eye. Mermaid's purse is a wonderfully apt term for the pouch-like leathery egg capsules of dogfish and rays. This one belonged to a lesser spotted dogfish and was green-brown in colour, rectangular and about 5cm long, with filamentous tendrils at each corner.

A member of the shark family, dogfish are common in our inshore waters, growing to over half-a-metre in length and living on the seabed where they feed upon crustaceans and other small marine creatures. Dogfish is not a name I particularly like, especially since the prefix dog in traditional nature nomenclature is often used in the sense that the species is inferior in some way, for example, the dog violet is so called because it is scentless. Nowadays, there is a trend to call this fish the small-spotted catshark, which has a much nicer ring to it. Nonetheless, I have always known this species as dogfish and find it difficult to change the habit.

As the eggs are deposited, the female dogfish repeatedly swims round an object such as a clump of seaweed, until the filaments of the capsule become entangled and firmly anchored to the seabed. Over the course of a few months the embryo gradually develops into a tiny baby dogfish, which will then break free from the protective casing. After stormy weather, the vacant egg cases are often washed ashore.

There was something different about this mermaid's purse lying on the shore of Wardie Bay. On holding the semi-transparent egg case up against the light of the sky, I could clearly see that there was a developing embryo dogfish curled up inside. Within this purse-like capsule was a beating piscine heart, a new life soon ready to emerge into the watery shallows of the Firth of Forth. In my hand was something truly special, a miracle of nature found lying by the edge of Scotland's capital city.

Chapter 7

PARADISE LAGOON AND FLOWERS OF THE SEA BREEZE

April 2021 – Elie and Earlsferry

Paradise Lagoon seems an entirely appropriate name to have coined for this large, shallow sea pool by the shore near Elie in the East Neuk of Fife. Exposed at extreme low tides, I had snorkelled in its languid expanses several times before, and from the first instance, the clarity of the water and abundance of sea life had brought me under its spell. Paradise? Yes, most definitely, and Paradise Lagoon has stuck in my mind ever since, despite the whimsical nature of this name conjured from the depths of the imagination.

Lady's Tower (East Neuk, Fife)

Situated under the shadow of the ruins of Lady's Tower, which was built in the eighteenth century for Lady Janet Anstruther, this lagoon is a treasure trove of underwater surprises. A narrow fissure in the rocks drains the lagoon into the open sea, yet the release of water is slow and only occurs at the lowest ebb of the tide. The placid stillness of the lagoon greatly aids the visibility, and whenever I have slipped through the rock gap into the choppier sea beyond, the water was less clear.

On one occasion when snorkelling in the lagoon, I inadvertently cornered a lobster by a rocky outcrop. With nowhere to go, the belligerent crustacean charged forward, waving its fearsome pincers in the process. This aggression, however, was all bluster and threat, and I was in little danger of being nipped. As the lobster neared my facemask, it delivered an agile sidestep, and the creature scuttled past and fled to the safety of deeper water.

So, it was with great anticipation that I plunged my wetsuit-clad body once more into this kelp-fringed lagoon on a frosty April morning, the water swirling past my mask in a flurry of sparkling bubbles. My vision quickly cleared to reveal a colourful underwater garden, carpeted with every type of seaweed imaginable.

It is easy to regard seaweeds as being simply brown or dull green, and not terribly exciting, but these were bright limey-green sea lettuces, the warm hues of purple-brown dulse, the reddish and leaf-like sea beech and the crinkly flattened fronds of sugar kelp. One particularly eye-catching type was a rock encrusting coral-like species, known as pink paint weed. It doesn't resemble a typical seaweed at all because its hard, chalky form coats rock surfaces like a pink rough-cast wall finish.

I was glad that this species had a common English everyday name for many species in the natural world do not, and are simply known by their Latin scientific nomenclatures. It may seem a moot point, but the lack of an easily identifiable name for individual species of flora, fauna and fungi diminishes our everyday recognition of more unusual lifeforms.

This was well illustrated when I glided into a margin of the lagoon, where a yellow-orange shimmering shone from a rock shelf. It was the delightfully named breadcrumb sponge, which displayed raised bumps and distinctive pores. Breadcrumb sponge – now, that is a name that sticks in the mind and is hard to forget.

This lagoon was as vibrant as any wildflower meadow, and in among the seaweed fronds, juvenile saithe and cod darted. Seaweeds are algae – simple and primitive plants – and they play a crucial role in the marine ecosystem, releasing oxygen through photosynthesis, as well as providing shelter for a multitude of creatures. Sponges, on the other hand, are sessile, filter feeding animals, which pass seawater through their pores while filtering out food particles.

There was much else to keep me preoccupied as casual flicks of my flippers propelled me slowly forward. Unusual greenish, gooseberry-like jelly blobs adorned many of the seaweed fronds, swaying and bobbing around in the gentle water movement. They were the eggs of green-leaf worms, spectacular emerald creatures that live in crevices, mussel beds and among kelp. It was an interesting quirk of nature how these worms, which are seldom seen, were revealing their presence so noticeably through this abundance of jellified egg mass balls.

The more I explored the shallow underwater haven, the more was revealed, and if one were to snorkel the lagoon a hundred times, each occasion would deliver a new surprise. Below me, the sand suddenly exploded into a cloud of sparkling grains as a large flounder bolted away. I had no inkling the flatfish was even there, such was its superb camouflage. This cryptic colouration was even more strikingly displayed by another flounder that appeared shortly afterwards. As the fish moved slowly over the seabed, it intermittently disappeared, merging seamlessly with the bottom by turning lighter to match sand, or slightly darker over stony ground. This flounder, and its capacity to blend with its environment, encapsulated the essence of nature and why it is so inspiring.

There were other fish about too, including attractive two-spotted gobies, which liked nothing better than to hang motionless in the water column, as well as fifteen-spined sticklebacks with their long and elegant bodies. Hermit crabs were abundant, scurrying along the bottom in their requisitioned whelk shells.

On a previous visit to this part of the shore, the strangest creature imaginable materialised, crawling slowly along the bottom, soft bodied and avocado green in colour, about 15cm long with two pairs of stubby tentacles on the top of the head. It was a sea hare and the first time I had ever seen one. The animal is so-called because, for those with an imaginative disposition, its front two tentacles can be likened to a hare's ears. The sea hare is a mollusc, but has no external shell, and when threatened by a predator, the animal releases a purple cloud of ink combined with a milky mix of chemicals that confuses the attacker. This was one of nature's most bizarre creations, a crawling soft mass, with fleshy 'wings', which are used to aid propulsion over the seabed. Sea hares that graze on red seaweeds are reddish, whilst those that do so on green seaweed are greenish.

Sea Hare

I snorkelled for a while longer, but with the air temperature not much above freezing, the cold soon got the better of me and I hauled myself out of the water, thrilled at the marine riches revealed once more within Paradise Lagoon. On tentatively making my way over slippery rocks back up the shore, it was impossible to resist the temptation of turning over some rocks to seek out the life lurking beneath. On lifting one flattish stone, a rockling – a ruddy, elongated fish – wriggled away, but it was too quick to catch.

The rocky exposed shore was a marvel of geology and nature with its broad sloping shelves that were deeply incised in places, revealing rock walls festooned with winkles, barnacles and anemones. My eyes were drawn to a scattering of limpets that clung with an iron grip to a huge boulder. It is not unusual for their incredibly strong rasping teeth to carve little circular depressions into rock surfaces. Limpet teeth are constructed from one of the strongest materials yet discovered in the natural world, rivalling even the toughest man-made equivalents.

Within the humble limpet shell, we can learn and harvest so much – for example, by mimicking their special tooth design engineers have been able to develop ultra-strong materials that benefit society. We also learn a valuable life lesson, for on every occasion a plant or animal becomes extinct, not only is it a tragic ecological loss and a moral outrage, but we also potentially lose an opportunity to deliver betterment for humanity.

The limpets were a fine example of natural endurance at its most impressive. The intertidal zone is a harsh and unforgiving environment, pounded by churning seas and exposed to huge environmental extremes. Whelks, winkles and limpets exposed to the summer noonday sun must positively bake inside their shells, yet only a few hours' later the cold sea envelops them again. In winter, they endure sharp frosts at low tide, and when the sea comes crashing back in, surging currents and huge waves threaten to dislodge them from their rocky homes. If all that were not enough, hordes of avian predators such as oystercatchers, curlews, turnstones and redshanks pick over the ground at low tide, while at high water, a new wave of predatory creatures sweep in, including cod and flounders. It is hard to think of any other habitat that undergoes so much daily variation.

Elie and the adjacent village of Earlsferry have many other natural attractions to offer. The previous day, I had taken the coastal cliff walk that heads westwards towards Shell Bay, beyond which lies the much larger expanse of Largo Bay. The Firth of Forth sparkled and danced under the spring sunshine, and when seen from the cliff above Earlsferry's West Bay, the sea had an almost Caribbean quality, with the turquoise water in the sandy shallows revealing the darker outlines of rocky reefs and banks of kelp.

On the south side of the Forth, the distinctive outline of the Bass Rock fore-dropped the conical hill of North Berwick Law in East Lothian, both of which are volcanic plugs. A pair of gannets flew past on purposeful, white-flashed wings, no doubt heading on their way to the Bass Rock where their breeding season was now getting under way. The gannets brought back fond memories of a visit to the Bass Rock a few years previously at the invitation of the Scottish Seabird Centre at North Berwick.

It was an unusual experience, for I had never been birdwatching with a 'riot shield'. Gannets are feisty birds, so everyone in the group was equipped with two hard plastic sheets as a means of protection. As we made our way up a narrow section of path on the Rock, the shields held on either side of our legs provided perfect protection from the mischievous pecks delivered by the dagger-like beaks of the bickering gannets protecting their ground nests.

The shields worked a treat and we soon reached a small plateau. It was a scene almost too much to behold – a maelstrom of noise and swirling gannets hanging in the sea breeze on stiffly held wings. And then there was the smell, the heavy aroma of fishy guano that enveloped the air like a seeping mist.

Spellbinding, mesmerising, awe-inspiring are all descriptions used with too much ease in our day-to-day language, but here on the world's largest gannet colony such terminology did apply, and truth be told, does little justice to the actuality.

Every conceivable space of rock was taken up by nesting gannets, stretching ahead of us in a sea of white. This was a place where a thousand dramas were being played out at the same time: gannets squabbling and beak stabbing with their neighbours while others were engaged in pair bonding ecstasy as they raised and shook their heads together in mutual affection.

There was also much plunder going on, whether it be sneaky gannets stealing seaweed from nearby nests so as top up their own or herring gulls swooping down to feast upon unguarded eggs.

Over 150,000 gannets nest on the Rock and they have been doing rather well in recent times with numbers increasing. Much of this success lies in their ability to hunt for a variety of fish species over large distances, meaning if fish are scarce in one area, they can find a hotspot somewhere else.

My mind turned back to the present once more, and as the pair of gannets disappeared out into the vastness of the Forth, the ground of this Earlsferry clifftop became a new focus of attention, for wildflowers abound on this stretch of the coast. Although it was still early in the season, there was much to appreciate, including cowslips that were beginning to emerge on a grassy margin. Related to the primrose, they are scarce wildflowers nowadays and seem to thrive best on these short-cropped coastal grasslands.

Especially abundant was scurvygrass, a straggly white-flowering perennial, which I had come across only a few weeks previously at Caerlaverock on the first stage of my nature journey. Captain Cook was a great advocate of this plant in ensuring the health of his crew because of its high Vitamin C content. I popped a leaf into my mouth, but it was bitter to the taste and had little to commend it.

Also showing well were the hazy rose-pink cushions of thrift, or sea-pink as it is sometimes known. It is one of our classic coastal flowers, and when examined up close, the petals reveal an intricate array of little pinkish frills. The narrow leaves are undistinguished and tight, probably to help conserve water in this place of persistent salt-laden winds and well-drained soils.

There were other gems, too, including the yellow, glowing orbs of early flowering rock-rose. It is not a rose at all, but a low creeping plant, often found on coastal grasslands and rocky places. After more wandering, I sat on a boulder to embrace the wildness. There was a flickering on the top of a wind-sculpted hawthorn, which turned out to be a male stonechat, his orange-glowed breast catching the spring sun. Stonechats are charming little birds, forever surveying the world from prominent perches, and uttering their distinctive grating 'tchak, tchak' calls.

The natural aura of the clifftop was empowering, but the hand of humankind was here too in the form of the remains of coastal gun emplacements from the Second World War. Three large calibre naval guns were sited here, along with observation posts, a reminder of the turmoil of the not-too-distant past, and perhaps even a dark and brooding forewarner of the uncertainties that remain with us even to this day.

Further eastwards up the coast lay Fife Ness, the easternmost tip of Fife, forming a headland that juts out into the North Sea. In my younger days, I adored visiting there in spring and autumn to seek out rare migrant songbirds. The area was productive for rarities, especially after a spell of strong easterly winds, which would blow eastern European migrants off-course to make their first landfall here. The Isle of May, which lies at the mouth of the Firth of Forth, is another spot renowned for rare migrants and is home to a bird ringing station where researchers can record and study their movements.

I recall seeing wrynecks, bluethroats, barred warblers and several other unusual species at Fife Ness. It was twitcher heaven, and undeniably exciting too, carefully examining scrubby areas in the hope of glimpsing something unusual. My twitching days are, however, over and now I get more enjoyment from observing the behaviour of our commoner bird species or seeking out insects, plants and intertidal life; a mellowing of the mind if you like, moving from the fast lane of ticking off new species to a more sedate and thoughtful approach to nature.

Chapter 8

LEGACY OF A ROYAL HUNTING FOREST

April 2021 – Glen Finglas

Natural history and human history often brush against one another. The Scottish landscape, for example, has many tales from the past to tell, such as ruined stone dwellings from the Highland Clearances and shallow ridges and undulations in the ground that mark old field systems.

Glen Finglas, which sits in the heart of Loch Lomond and the Trossachs National Park, is a case in point and from my vantage point overlooking the Finglas Water near Brig o' Turk, the tumbling rapids and pools below caused their own stir back in the nineteenth century. In 1853, John Ruskin had commissioned artist John Everett Millais to paint a combined landscape and portraiture that they envisaged would revolutionise British art. Millais was a rising star of the Pre-Raphaelite Brotherhood, whereas Ruskin – whilst an accomplished painter himself – felt his talents lay in identifying and revealing the greatness of others, and Millais was his latest protégé.

The pair – who at this time were friends – carefully chose this spot in Glen Finglas for the painting, which Ruskin described as, 'a lovely piece of worn rock, with foaming water and weeds'. Ruskin was to stand looking contemplatively down the swirling and gushing burn, whilst Millais's skilled brush strokes captured both the spirit of the man and the drama of the surrounding wildness.

Ruskin proved a hard taskmaster and he continually criticised the progress of Millais's endeavours over the months that followed, resulting in the painting having to be repeatedly altered. It must have been an incredibly difficult period for Millais, but from such frustration he soon found solace in Ruskin's attractive wife, Effie Gray (named Euphemia, she is always known as Effie) which resulted in an affair that would eventually lead to marriage. Ruskin appeared largely indifferent to the dalliance, although his subsequent annulment caused much scandal at the time.

The painting today has huge resonance in the art world, vividly portraying the character of one of the Victorian era's most influential thinkers and which also has indelibly embossed upon it a most remarkable love story. The exact spot of the painting was rediscovered in 1993 and Woodland Trust Scotland (WTS), which owns and manages Glen Finglas, has created a short trail that leads to the spot.

I enjoy visiting wild places with stories to divulge, so I lingered for a while, conjuring in my mind images of not just Ruskin and Millais, but also the many other people from the even more distant past who must have once stood on the ground beneath my feet. Time has brought about hugely significant change to the landscape, with the Finglas Water having been dammed in the 1960s, a short distance upstream from where Millais painted Ruskin, creating a reservoir that dominates the glen. As I made my way up to the reservoir, the signs of spring were all around: a male chaffinch sang from the branch of a birch tree and glowing primroses brought vibrant colour to the ground.

Chaffinches are one of Scotland's most beautiful birds, yet because they are so common, there is a tendency to overlook them. As such, I consciously made the decision to pause in my tracks to give this singing male the appreciation he deserved. It was a simple song, lacking the depth and variation found in other birds. Describing bird song with the written word is challenging, but Thomas Coward, the twentieth-century ornithologist, summed up the uncomplicated melody of the chaffinch perfectly when he wrote:

The rollicking song, often begun in February, is a rattle with an exuberant ending, which, however, varies, not only in different localities, but individually.

Thomas Coward, *Birds of the British Isles and their Eggs* (1969)

The fact that chaffinches have individual personalities and slightly varying songs depending on location was an interesting observation, and certainly not something I have ever discerned. Gilbert White, the eighteenth-century nature diarist, was similarly intrigued by the subtle variations in the call of the tawny owl. In his seminal book, *Natural History and Antiquities of Selborne* (1789), White noted:

*My musical friend, at whose house I am now visiting, has
tried all the owls that are his near neighbours with a pitch-
pipe set at concert pitch, and finds that they all hoot in B flat.*

White recounted later instances of other owls hooting in different keys
wondering, 'Do these different notes proceed from different species, or
only from various individuals?'

Taking the time and patience to observe in detail the creatures around
us is the hallmark of a good naturalist, and both White and Coward held
such qualities in abundance. My focus turned once more to the chaffinch
on the branch above me, but he had become ill at ease by my near presence,
or perhaps had become tired of singing, for he abruptly flitted away in an
undulating flight.

A short time later, the vast open sweep of the glen unfolded before me,
a hauntingly picturesque panorama of the sparkling reservoir encircled by
brooding hills. Just as how history had touched the Finglas Water below
the reservoir, this too was a landscape steeped in sagas, with the proximity
of the ancient centres of power at Stirling and Doune resulting in it
becoming a Royal hunting forest popular with Scottish kings from the
early 1300s until the 1700s. Characterised by a mix of trees, hill and open
ground, it is a varied habitat that benefits wildlife to this day.

Most notably, Glen Finglas is characterised by nationally scarce 'wood
pasture' – upland that has been managed for many centuries with grazing
animals, along with the cutting or 'pollarding' of hazels and alders. WTS
is working to restore and further enhance this open ancient woodland
through tree planting and careful management, including controlled
grazing. Over one million native trees have been planted in the glen, and
WTS is working with other partners as part of the Great Trossachs Forest
National Nature Reserve to restore the landscape to a natural mix of
moorland, wetland and native woodland.

One bird which especially benefits from this patchwork is the black
grouse, which is much scarcer than the red grouse so commonly seen on
Scottish moorlands. I scoured the trees and ground with my binoculars in
the hope of glimpsing one but the search proved frustratingly fruitless. I
drew solace in the recollection from a few years previously when WTS had
invited me to Glen Finglas to participate in a dawn black grouse safari to

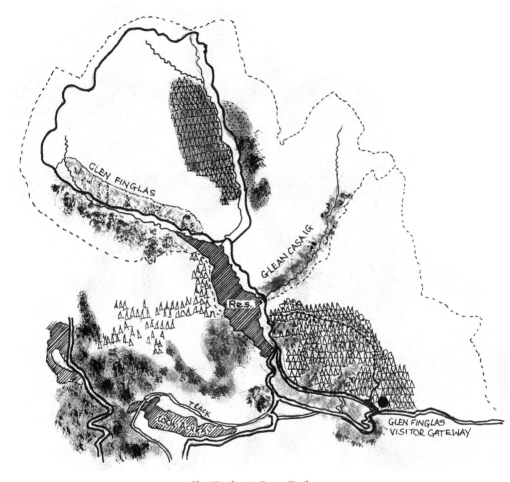

Glen Finglas & Forest Trails

witness their spectacular courtship behaviour, known as lekking. Black grouse leks are traditional courting grounds where the males dance, croon and fight with each other as they seek to impress the females watching nearby. That early morning in Glen Finglas was a wonderful experience, with the male blackcocks constantly squaring up to one another, and filling the air with their hypnotic warbling croons that resonated from deep within their vibrating throats. Interspersed between the softer notes were frequent sharp hisses, a signal of the seriousness of intent, which is to drive off rival blackcocks and to mate with as many hens as possible.

Black Grouse lekking (Glen Finglas)

With that previous black grouse encounter still prevailing strong across my mind, I ventured further up the glen. A short while later, a raven swept low over the brow of the ridge on black, wind-tumbled wings and disappeared over another hill crest. I wondered what the nobility, who once hunted this land, thought about the ravens they must have frequently encountered.

Raven (Glen Finglas)

It was an interesting question for ravens have been both reviled and revered, but mostly the former, from early historical times, with the bird inextricably associated with ill fortune, suspicion and fear. Much of this notoriety stems around the belief that ravens are never far away whenever there is the hint of a carcass to feast upon.

Shakespeare's *Macbeth* refers to a raven croaking himself hoarse on the fatal entrance of Duncan; and King Kenneth I of Scotland was hailed as the 'raven feeder' in reference to the bodies of his opponents left behind on the field of battle. This is no doubt the reason why marauding Vikings so eagerly welcomed the appearance of ravens as an omen of victory during conflict. With its formidable thickset beak, the raven is certainly a prolific scavenger and, in Scotland, has long benefited from the constant availability of sheep and deer carcasses on our hillsides.

If the chaffinch is ubiquitous in our woodlands and hedgerows, the meadow pipit is equally so on moorland and hill. As I retraced my steps back to Brig o' Turk, several swept up before me, their thin piping calls filling the air. The raven appeared once more above the ridge before slipping over the far side, a dark sentinel of this wild landscape and a reminder of the turbulent past, when its presence would have instilled a sense of foreboding in the hearts and minds of our ancestors.

Chapter 9

STRIKING BUTTERFLIES
AND INDUSTRIOUS BEAVERS

April 2021 – Central Perthshire

There was a fluttering by the track edge on the moors north of Dunkeld that was so small and insignificant it barely registered upon my mind. Perhaps it was a flicker of the imagination, but curiosity took grip, so I scrambled down a small incline to investigate this movement.

Up into the air flitted a little moth-like creature, before swiftly alighting on a grass stem, closing its wings to reveal the most stunning emerald-green colour imaginable. It was a green hairstreak butterfly, a scarce species that is a joy to find especially as they are easy to miss because of their diminutive size.

Green Hairstreak

The brightness of the emerald underwings is so striking, that, once seen, it remains indelibly imprinted upon the mind. In some ways this is a butterfly in reverse because the upper sides of the wings are brown and unremarkable, and it is only the underparts that are so eye-catching. Compared to many other Scottish butterflies, green hairstreaks have a short flight period, only being on the wing from late April until early June.

They are fussy in their requirements, preferring sunny sheltered sites in open birch woodland, forest clearings and moorland, where blaeberry is found – the food plant of their caterpillars.

Shortly after glimpsing the green hairstreak, a peacock butterfly floated past like an autumnal wind-blown leaf, held aloft on fragile burgundy wings. Peacocks are one of our most beautiful butterflies, but they are flighty and often frustrating to watch as they never stay still for any length of time, settling briefly before spiralling up into the air once more. When one does eventually alight for a while, the wonderfully patterned wings shine out, most notably the four false 'eyes', one in each corner. Nature is unrivalled in its intricacy and purpose of design, and these big 'eyes' are a clever ruse to scare birds and other predators. In effect, the peacock is pretending to be a bug-eyed monster, a case of beauty and the beast wrapped together in a colourful cloak.

Unlike the green hairstreak, peacocks are long-lived, and many survive from July until the following May. During winter they hibernate in sheltered sites such as garden sheds, stone walls or outhouses. Prior to hibernation, peacocks gorge themselves on late season nectar and will seek out rotten windfall apples to sup upon their life-enhancing sugary sweetness. Despite this fattening up, it is hard to comprehend how such a vulnerable, paper-thin creature can endure our coldest months, and many succumb over winter. For those that do survive until spring, it becomes a race against time to find other peacocks with which to mate to ensure the creation of the next generation.

This vast and intricate tapestry of open moor, forest and lochs that stretches from Dunkeld to Pitlochry is one of my favoured stomping grounds. I have seen eight species of bird of prey here, including golden eagle and hen harrier, watched adders bask on sunny banks, and on two separate occasions glimpsed stoats in their full white winter ermine coats bounding across paths.

Perthshire lies at the heart of Scotland, a vast county that stretches from the fringes of the Cairngorms in the north to the subtle undulating beauty of the Ochil Hills much further to the south. It is sometimes dubbed Big Tree Country because of its towering firs. The botanist and collector, David Douglas, who was born in Scone, travelled around North America in the nineteenth century seeking out new tree species to introduce to

Scotland, including the Douglas fir, which is named after him. While Big Tree Country is an entirely appropriate term for Perthshire, Big River Country is arguably a more apt description, for the River Tay is the artery of life that dominates the county's soul, and from which a multitude of other rivers drain into. These are no miniscule rivers either, but mighty ones in their own right – the Tummel, Earn, Ericht, Garry and Isla to name but a few. There are many smaller ones too, such as the Ardle and Bruar, each one special and unique in character.

Inevitably, these rivers have left an imprint upon our culture. North beyond Pitlochry, for example, on the Bruar Water lie the picturesque Bruar Falls, which Robert Burns visited in 1786. He found the falls wondrously beautiful but lamented that their 'effect was much impaired by the want of shrubs and trees'. This inspired him to write 'The Humble Petition of Bruar Water', which resulted in the Fourth Duke of Atholl planting larch and Scots pines on the land thus transforming the surrounding environment.

An intricate mosaic of lochs and lochans dot this Perthshire landscape, and one of the largest is Loch Ordie, which I reached after a couple of hours from the start of my walk at the Atholl Estates car park, a short distance from Dunkeld. On the final approach, an osprey on wide but slender wings swept up from a pine by the loch's edge, rippling out a musical 'pew, pew, pew'. The call of an osprey has a tone and resonance reminiscent of a green woodpecker, a lovely and repetitive ringing that epitomises the wildness of the land. This osprey veered around a stand of pines, its white underwings and belly briefly catching the light, before heading southwards, probably towards the nearby Rotmell and Dowally Lochs in its quest for trout.

I skirted the west side of Loch Ordie, and then took a track down a shallow glen, following the course of the Buckny Burn, before striking along a narrow, grassy path that skirts the southern fringe of Deuchary Hill. Here, a small group of fallow deer grazed on a section of open land, including a hind with a startling creamy-white coat, which shone out like a beacon. White fallows are not unusual, and rather than being albinos, this is a naturally occurring coat anomaly. Fallows, in general, show much colour variation, some being dark and others a softer, dappled fawn. Standing out from the crowd is not normally a recipe for survival in the wild, but there are no significant natural predators for deer here, enabling the snowy-white animals to thrive.

Although I had tried to blend inconspicuously by crouching low behind a heathery hummock, this little group of deer were spooked by my near presence, and they bounded up to a hill crest, then paused momentarily, where the white individual glowed and shimmered like a silver ghost illuminated under the low evening sun. The deer slipped over the far side of the ridge and the hillside fell empty once more.

Fallows are native to Continental Europe and were first introduced into Scotland as park deer in the thirteenth century. They are patchily distributed, with one of their main strongholds being Highland Perthshire. Fallows are surprisingly sedentary, and as far as I am aware, the Perthshire deer have not spread to adjacent parts of the country and are seemingly content to roam their core area.

Black-Headed Gull (Mill Dam, Dunkeld)

A short while later, I arrived at Mill Dam, a silver-speckled lochan where black-headed gulls nested in the recent past but, sadly, no longer do so. Although gulls have a reputation for brashness and gluttony, black-headed gulls are softer and more benign in their nature. They are elegant and often hawk above rivers and lochs for hatching insects like giant, graceful swallows, swerving and cavorting in the air with surprising agility. Their vulnerability lies during the breeding season when they nest by the marshy margins of lochs, for it just takes one fox or pine marten to brave the boggy ground to create havoc by snatching eggs or chicks.

With our wetlands forever diminishing, I fear for the future of black-headed gulls, given that there are fewer places for them to safely nest. 'Rewilding' is the current buzzword in nature conservation, and restoring impoverished habitat is key for the future prosperity of our native flora and fauna. If the land is lush with a sustainable mix of forest, bog, meadows and farmland, then an enhanced natural equilibrium is achieved, which benefits all of nature, including the breeding fortunes of black-headed gulls.

Rewilding also means beavers, and while the black-headed gulls have gone from Mill Dam, these large and intriguing rodents have become firmly established here. Their signs were everywhere, including channels cut into the shore edges and through the mats of vegetation, as well as birches and willows felled on the bankside. Out on the water, and scattered among the marginal wetland plants, were piles of branches collected by their industry – food stores for a rainy day.

Beaver (Mill Dam, Dunkeld)

The large size of some of the trees felled was impressive, bordering on the improbable, given the girth of the trunks that had been gnawed through. Depending on the season, beavers feed on bark, twigs, leaves and water plants and Mill Dam must be a rather noisy place at night as trees continually crash to the ground. Mill Dam is the equivalent of beaver Nirvana, and my immediate thought was that this was like a wild scene straight from the Canadian Rockies. Better than that, this was wild Caledonia and before my eyes lay a watery beaver-engineered landscape last witnessed by our forebears several hundred years ago when the animals still roamed the land and before they were hunted to extinction. Nature had crafted this landscape and I felt uplifted by it all.

Although dusk was gathering pace, venturing homewards was the last thing on my mind, and the beaver activity so engrossing that I lingered for a while longer, wandering round to the northern fringes of the loch where there is a broad, flat, grassy expanse, comprising part bog, part drier ground. Beaver-felled trees scattered the area, despite being a reasonable distance from the open water of the loch. Beavers are reluctant to wander any great distance from water, so how did they access this area? I soon found the answer – a channel created by the enlargement of a narrow, slow flowing burn. The beavers had widened it into a swimmable waterway, and then dammed another section to create an even larger expanse of water above, where they could feed and swim in safety. It was a remarkable feat, and an intelligent one too, with the animals having worked-out within their minds how to expand their range into new foraging areas.

Beavers are controversial in Scotland and sometimes come into conflict with farming and other landowning interests for a variety of reasons, including blocking drainage ditches and damaging crops. In upland Perthshire, however, the ecological benefits brought by beavers are overwhelming, given that the pond created above the dam held a cornucopia of invertebrate and plant life. This was a place where pond skaters glided across the surface, and water beetles and caddisfly and mayfly larva (nymphs) abounded below. A sceptic might point to the numerous felled trees as ecological vandalism, and I recall several years previously talking to a walker here, who was so bemused by the 'damage' wreaked that he thought the beavers should be controlled.

I understood where he was coming from, yet initial appearances are one thing; much better to look closer to appreciate the fuller story. Many of the felled trees are in effect coppiced rather than killed and will spawn new green shoots of recovery. There is also a tendency to be overly precious about woodland trees because the most diverse parts of forests are invariably the clearings and glades where the sun can filter through to the ground below. In such places, wildflowers prosper, attracting bumblebees, butterflies, moths and other pollinators. Tumbled trees will also slowly rot, providing refuge and places to reproduce for a host of other invertebrates and fungi. Beavers often fell trees into rivers so that they can feed at leisure from the safety of the water. When this happens, the half-submerged branches form the equivalent of ocean reefs, providing shelter for trout and minnows as well as invertebrates. Tree felling by beavers has been ingrained in the natural order since the dawn of time, ensuring a diverse environment that supports more life than would otherwise be possible without these dynamic wild foresters. Beavers paddled the waterways long before intensive farming ever became part of the scene, and perhaps we should remember that whenever the instinct for control is considered.

Darkness was taking hold, and it was a 40-minute walk back to the car park, so I reluctantly departed Mill Dam, treading with cautious footsteps along the track under the diminishing light. A ghostly barn owl floated over a distant field until I lost sight of it by the shadows of a stand of trees. Pipistrelle bats flickered overhead on fast-beating wings, tumbling and undulating as if out of control. The gentle breeze had eased, and now the stillness of the night was all empowering. Another wave of creatures was emerging – badgers, foxes and pine martens – and although I could not see them, my mind conjured their presence. The silent, languid air had taken grip and the only sound was the gentle pad of my footsteps; one man and the night, and it was wonderfully addictive.

Chapter 10

MYSTERIOUS CUCKOOS AND CLOSE ENCOUNTERS WITH BEAVERS

May 2021 – Duror and Appin

It was a natural scene of intriguing incongruity: the temperature was barely five degrees centigrade and fresh spring snow dusted the hill tops of Appin, and yet a cuckoo newly arrived from the dark and impenetrable forests of central Africa was calling its celebration to a Scottish May. The cuckoo's call is such a hypnotic and entrancing sound – 'coo-koo, coo-koo' – a wild and echoing resonance, with a pitch and tone that easily drifts for a couple of kilometres, especially within the imposing amphitheatre of a Highland glen.

The frigid air suggested winter, but the heart of spring was all around at the foot of Glen Duror, including willow warblers delivering their sweet cascading songs and swallows weaving over nearby sheep pasture. Cold springs are an ever-present hazard for early arriving migrant birds, but on this bitter morning by the village of Duror, the warblers, sand martins and swallows were as active as ever, shrugging-off such inclemency with apparent ease. I suspected, nonetheless, they were struggling to find insect food and survival depended on the temperature rising over the following days.

It was the cuckoo, though, that captured my senses more than anything else. Its flute-like call penetrated every fold and gully of the hillside like a creeping mist, an evolutionary adaption that maximises the chances of attracting a female. The cuckoo paused and called again, a seemingly benign and haunting deliverance, but one that potentially sounds the death knell for the soon-to-hatch chicks of some unlucky ground-nesting meadow pipits.

Once mated, the female cuckoo will seek a secluded look-out perch and patiently wait, perhaps for hours at a time, scanning the hillside with coiled predatory instinct, ready to unleash herself should she detect the tell-tale movement of an adult pipit. Even the tiniest pipit flicker is enough to alert the cuckoo to the location of its nest hidden in a grassy tussock.

Cuckoo (Glen Duror, Appin)

Then, down she swoops to devour one of the pipit eggs and lay her own ticking time-bomb replacement. In the blink of an eye, the piratical deed is committed; speed is essential so as not to arouse suspicion among the parent pipits. Shortly after hatching, the baby cuckoo will push the pipit chicks or unhatched eggs out from the nest, so that the imposter now has the full attention of its unwitting foster parents.

A female cuckoo has the capability to lay each of her eggs in a dozen or more individual pipit nests, and once the dark task is completed, she will up-wings and be gone by the middle of July, heading back to the lush forests of central Africa. It is a truly remarkable piece of natural history, but even more astonishing is how the baby cuckoos, once reared by their pipit foster-parents, know where to migrate to for the winter. There are no adults to follow and learn from, instead through a complex innate programme wired into their genes, they just head south and unerringly arrive in central Africa.

When one analyses cuckoos, an avalanche of biological questions and thoughts spring forth. For example, how did their unusual breeding strategy evolve? And how is it that their eggs have similar colouration to that of their hosts? (Cuckoos which specialise upon meadow pipits have matching dark eggs, whilst those in other parts of Europe that prey upon redstarts lay blue eggs.)

I had much opportunity for such reflection in Duror as I had just acquired a second-hand touring caravan, which provided the perfect mobile base for the next stage of my Scottish wildlife odyssey, offering the opportunity to spend more time in areas further afield and come under their full natural spell. Duror, which lies between Oban and Fort William on the west coast mainland, is a place I had only passed through before, but now it had become an area of concentrated focus, and the calling cuckoo had sent my mind buzzing.

Climate change is resulting in many birds nesting earlier. It remains to be seen if cuckoos are able to adapt to such upheaval. If they arrive in Scotland a week or more after meadow pipits have laid all their eggs and started incubation, then the optimum moment for their own egg laying is missed. How can cuckoos wintering in the swamp and river forests of Cameroon, the Democratic Republic of Congo, Gabon and Angola anticipate such climatic flux and the subtle changes in meadow pipit nesting behaviour in a land several thousand kilometres away? I am not sure they can, and that is a real worry, especially since the cuckoo is but one of a multitude of species that face such challenges. Timing is everything in nature, from blue tits ensuring that their chicks hatch at peak caterpillar abundance to ensure a plentiful food supply, to moths that emerge and breed when key food plants are flourishing. If the timing goes wrong, the creation of future generations of life is blown askew.

Ardsheal is a small bump of land that encroaches into Loch Linnhe, and for me, was the centrepiece attraction of the area around Duror. I spent several days exploring its wild shoreline and wonderful mixed deciduous woods, principally of oak, birch and hazel. One cold afternoon, I even took a dip with snorkel and mask into the picturesque Cuil Bay but strangely did not see any fish. I do not recall that ever happening during a west coast snorkel before. That is often the way when observing nature, sometimes no matter how hard one seeks one type of creature, it fails to materialise. I consoled myself with other interesting discoveries, including a comb jelly – an almost transparent gelatinous creature, about the size of a large grape, and with little paddling combs radiating around its body that caught the light like a sparkling rainbow. The apparent lack of fish was a case of bad luck on my part, for once I had splashed out of the water, a pair of fish-eating, red-breasted mergansers glided close to the pebbly shore, and further out, a shag repeatedly dived under the waves. The fish were there, my underwater spotting skills were not.

On another day, I struck north from Duror along the Oban to Fort William cycle path and then followed the coast of Ardsheal from Kentallen in a looping return circuit that brought me back to Cuil Bay on the southern fringe. It is a lovely walk, with the mountains of Morvern on the opposite side of Loch Linnhe providing an impressive backdrop. Cuckooflower was in full spectacular bloom, which was most appropriate, given the calling cuckoos. The flowers can vary from almost white to deep mauve, and according to John Gerard, the sixteenth-century herbalist, the plant is so named because it blooms 'for the most part in April and May, when the cuckoo begins to sing her pleasant note without stammering'.

The woodland that sloped down upon the approach lane to the imposing Ardsheal House was ablaze with primroses, dog violets and wood sorrel, providing a complementary artistic canvas of yellows, purples and whites. There was something intrinsically beguiling about this wood, so I ventured up a deer path and quickly became besotted by its twisted branches and moss-covered stumps. A tumbled oak trunk provided a welcome platform to rest, so I sat for a while, breathing in the quiet solitude of what is effectively a temperate rainforest. The aura here was bordering on the primeval: silent air and patterns of grey, brown and the emerging limey-green leaves of spring.

This was a moisture-laden environment rich in ferns and mosses, and liverworts, which are simple plants that thrive in the humidity and shade. Small ferns clung to mossy trunks like tropical rainforest epiphytes; honeysuckles weaved their intricate tendrils through hazel margins, just as how creeping lianas would in a South American jungle. I examined the decomposing oak trunk around me and noticed it was covered in a strange-looking grey mat of dog-tooth lichen, which is so-called because its brownish fruiting spores bear a passing resemblance to dog teeth. Lichens are like mosses, all around us yet seldom remarked upon. They are one of our more fascinating lifeforms, for they consist of two (or more) organisms rather than one. It is a concept I find difficult to get my head around. In simple terms, lichens are partnerships between algae and fungi in which the organisms are so closely interwoven they appear as one.

It is a mutually beneficial relationship where the algae produce food through photosynthesis while the fungi use their inherent properties to create structural support, as well to provide mineral nutrients and to store water to prevent desiccation. Although the numerous types of lichens that occur are classed as individual species, they are technically a combination of more than one. Lichens are incredibly successful and thrive in some of the most inhospitable places on earth. Climb to the top of the Cairngorms and there will be colourful lichens on the rocks. They are also common on boulders by the seashore, where some are tolerant of salt spray and brief immersion in saltwater. On the tidal margins of Ardsheal, there was a proliferation of a species known as yellow scale or shore lichen, which encrusted rocks in a fiery orange-yellow carpet.

The lichens were fascinating, but so too was the broad circumference of the decaying oak trunk I was resting upon. I pressed my right forefinger into it and the soft, damp wood yielded under the gentle pressure leaving a shallow indentation. Death delivers life, for where trees have been felled by ferocious storms or succumbed to age or disease, the resultant deadwood becomes one of our most important and diverse habitats. Inside this wood-decaying trunk, many specialised invertebrates prospered. I could not see them, but I knew they were there, and that was all that mattered, which gave me a strange sense of satisfaction. Various rare types of insect are dependent upon deadwood for their survival, including beetles, hoverflies and sawflies. Deadwood aids carbon capture and boosts the soil nutrient cycle, slowly releasing nitrogen back into the environment. A forest without deadwood is not a fully functioning natural forest at all, but a mere shadow of what it could potentially be.

The salty sea breeze eventually lifted me from the throes of contemplation, and not long after, I ventured down to the nearby rocky shore. A wader, which resembled a curlew, moved erratically on fast-pattering feet by the sea edge. Once brought under the scrutiny of my binoculars, I realised it was a whimbrel, which is similar to a curlew, but noticeably smaller, with the bill curved much steeper downwards at the tip. The call of the whimbrel is markedly different from that of a curlew, and when it took to the air, a high-pitched whinnying drifted over the shoreline. This whimbrel was on migration, heading north from its West African wintering grounds to breeding areas that encompass the Shetland Islands, Iceland, Scandinavia and the Faroes. Whimbrels have traditional staging posts where they pause to rest and feed when on migration. Unlike the pre-programmed migratory instincts of cuckoos, adult whimbrels pass the knowledge of resting places onto the next generation during group migrations.

As I approached the southern headland of Rubha Mor, a noticeable northwards movement of whimbrels materialised, the birds flying over the sea in small groups. They were funnelling into Loch Linnhe, before continuing their journey north-eastwards along Loch Ness and out into the Moray Firth and the North Sea beyond. From there, they would embark on the final stages of their epic northwards trek. Just as boats use the conduit of the Caledonian Canal and Loch Ness as a short-cut from the west to the east coast, so too do the whimbrels.

Ardsheal is interesting because along the shore are several distinctive raised beaches, creating broad, grassy flat expanses, grazed by sheep and cattle. A raised beach was once a proper sea-lapped beach, but due to fluctuations in sea level or uplifts of the land, it now lies above the current shore. On the rougher, heathery margins, the soft purple glimmering of lousewort beamed out. This low and attractive ground-hugging wildflower is so called because it was once thought that sheep that grazed on it suffered from lice and rarely prospered. The connection was correct but the reasoning not, for lousewort was merely an indicator rather than a cause. Lousewort thrives on poor, mineral-deficient soil, thus the poorly sheep were due to unproductive grazing caused by the barren soil, rather than any direct impact inflicted by the lousewort.

Sometimes when nature watching, the truly special happens. The day after my woodland excursion at Ardsheal, I felt compelled to revisit once more to gain a greater understanding of the oaks, birches and hazels, and the numerous types of other life they support. I was about to strike up into the wood, when out of habit, I scanned the adjacent open waters of Loch Linnhe with my binoculars. In the far distance, two dots bobbed in the water. They were birds, I envisaged. I checked them out further. One of the creatures dived under, revealing a distinctive sharp tail that momentarily pointed skywards – otters!

This pair were disappearing fast around a distant headland, so out of hope more than expectation, I abandoned my woodland foray and headed down to the pebbly beach, trotting as quickly possible to the headland. On reaching it, and about 200m out from the shore, I picked the otters up once more. Both dived before quickly resurfacing in a sparkling swirl of water. One had caught a flounder, and now both were powering through the sea like mini torpedoes right towards me to land their catch. They bounded onto the rocky shore edge only a short distance away and I could not believe my luck.

As they fed hungrily upon the flatfish, I crept closer still, until the gleam of their eyes and water-ruffled coats glinted under the warm sunshine. As this pair were sharing the fish, it seemed most likely this was a mother and her well-matured cub. It is the norm for cubs to remain with their mothers for up to a year, providing the opportunity to hone their fish-catching skills. After devouring the fish, the otters rested for a while in a shallow depression among the rocks, where they basked in the sunshine, the mother rolling on her side in lazy contentment.

Otter (Loch Linnhe)

Then the animals were away once more, but rather than fishing the deeper water as before, they worked the shallows right by the shore edge, swimming and undulating through the bladder wrack and other seaweeds. I walked parallel to them as they swam and dived along the beach, yet they completely ignored me. I knew they had seen me because when they were previously resting, they had occasionally glanced in my direction, sizing me up. I have witnessed such casual behaviour before with river-living otters – give them space, and they will tolerate you. Besides, such is their agility in the water, otters know the near proximity of a human poses them little threat.

This shallow water, almost beachcombing-like hunting technique, was proving productive, and on several occasions, one or other of the otters veered back to the shore to devour its catch, which mostly comprised of eel-like rocklings and butterfish. The otters were ambushing the fish by surprise, using their large whiskers as sensory touch receptors for finding them in among the thick, green tangles of seaweed. The same technique was probably used for the flounder that had been caught earlier. I know from my snorkelling experience that flounders typically lie motionless on the seabed, relying on cryptic camouflage to avoid detection, but once spooked, will shoot away like an explosive underwater missile. An otter must have lightning reflexes to snap up fish such as flounders before they bolt.

The mother and cub otter then went their separate ways, more by accident than design, the youngster returning along the route it had come, the mother continuing further along the shore. The cub soon realised it was on its own, and began to call, a sharp, piercing whistle. This was an anxious plea: 'Where are you, mother, where have you gone?' There was no reply and I too had lost sight of her. Suddenly, I felt like an intruder in their own private world, and tears welled in my eyes. My emotions surged with an intensity that surprised and shocked me in equal measure. I looked up towards the opposite shore or Morvern, and the towering, brooding hulk of the rocky mountain top of Beinn Mheadhoin. The rippling waves gently caressed the shore by my feet and a pair of oystercatchers piped up. My tearful eyes quickly transformed into sparkling contentment. Scotland's wild allure had taken grip in a way I had not previously thought possible – a tightening that would never relinquish.

Now was the time to go, to leave these wonderful animals in peace. As I turned on my heels, the young otter whistled once more, its haunting cry drifting along the wild shore of Loch Linnhe.

Chapter 11

WAILING DIVERS AND A SINGING BEACH

May 2021 – Camusdarach and Loch Shiel

The sweet aroma of coconut wafted through the air – the delicious scent of the bright yellow flowers of gorse that gleamed and smouldered in the spring sunshine by the sand-dunes at Camusdarach Beach, which lies between Arisaig and Mallaig.

Gorse flowers are dazzling, and it is said the pioneering eighteenth-century Swedish botanist, Carl Linnaeus, fell on his knees and wept the first time he encountered gorse in its full blooming glory. Although not universally loved, gorse is important to our environment, not least in providing useful nesting sites for linnets and whinchats. In winter, their flowers attract early pollinating insects. There is an old country saying that goes along the lines of, 'when gorse is out of bloom, kissing is out of season', a reflection of the fact that at least a few of its vibrant yellow flowers are likely to be in bloom, no matter the time of year.

Gorse

On one bare, dead gorse branch I discovered the encrusting, jellified mass of yellow brain fungus, its intricate folds and tucks resembling the structure of an animal's brain. Fungi have complex life histories and yellow brain fungus is no exception. This colourful species does not gain sustenance directly from the wood of gorse or other trees and bushes as one might expect, but instead feeds directly upon a wood-rotting crust fungus that also lives on decaying branches. It is difficult to comprehend how such an unusual interaction could have ever evolved. Why specialise in being a parasite upon a specific type of fungus? Such questions on evolution apply to virtually every part of nature, as I had only so recently discovered with the cuckoos in Appin. On thinking about the conundrum further, this adaptation probably evolved because the wood-rotting fungus engages in all the hard work in extracting nutrients from the branch, while the yellow brain takes the easy option by tapping into the ready-made food source of its host fungus.

Camusdarach is one of Scotland's most spectacular beaches, a white sandy sweep with crystal clear, turquoise water. Beyond the main beach further south, there are several sandy bays, each one a treasure trove of life. Out at sea, the horizon is dominated by the long flat plateau of the island of Eigg, with the prominent top of An Sgùrr breaking the skyline like a shark's fin. The mountains of Rum also loom large, as do the dark, serrated peaks of the Cuillin mountains of Skye.

Some plants are incredibly hardy, and no more so than the little, crimson-tinged English stonecrops that were secreted in cracks in the rocks close to the tideline. They are interesting plants, the succulent waxy-leaves designed to maximise water retention in this harsh, wind-blown, and salt-laden environment. Nearby, on the sandy shore, nestled the washed-up half-shell of an ocean quahog, a most mysterious clam. The shell was large, about the size of the palm of my hand, and was purple-brown in colouration with paler patches in the centre. These lighter hues are where the true shell pigment has been eroded over the course of time.

Ocean quahogs live below the low tide mark buried in the sand. In 2006, a specimen trawled up by Icelandic researchers was estimated to be 507 years old. In other words, it was born in 1499, only a few years after Columbus first sailed to the Americas, making these clams one of our longest living creatures. On picking up the quahog shell, it felt as if a priceless antique was cradled within my palm, and I pondered how old this one was and what historical events had passed over its lifetime. Nature never ceases to amaze me, so, with a degree of reverence, I gently laid the empty shell back down onto the dazzling white sand.

A group of half-a-dozen great northern divers busily fished offshore. They were absorbing to watch, especially since each time the birds dived under the water, they did so together as a unified team. I have observed this type of behaviour with other diving birds such as mergansers and have concluded it is a hunting technique that increases the chances of catching fish by covering the seabed in a broad sweep, stirring up creatures like a fishing trawl.

The divers were accomplished fishers and were able to stay submerged for a long time. On several occasions, I counted the duration of their dives, which was often for more than a minute, and never shorter than 40 seconds. Equally intriguing was the subtle way they submerged. Seabirds such as shags and cormorants dive under in a rolling flourish; the great northern divers at Camusdarach vanished beneath the waves like little sinking submarines, leaving barely a ripple behind.

As the divers fished, their haunting, long-drawn out cries occasionally drifted across the sea breeze, imparting an eerie, almost ghost-like quality. Great northern divers are called common loons in North America and it was entirely possible that some of the divers at Camusdarach would shortly be migrating to Canada for the breeding season (they also nest in Iceland and Greenland). This sparked another question. The inshore waters of north-west Scotland and the abundant lochs and lochans in the surrounding hills look perfect for great northern divers for breeding in the summer, so why do they migrate so far away to nest? It was hard to develop a rational answer, except perhaps that such migratory habits are a product of the past when environmental conditions were different. It is possible there are other indiscernible environment factors existing today, which precludes them from breeding in Scotland. If so, it highlights how fragilely balanced our environment is, with subtle nuances continually at work of which we are totally unaware.

Red-throated and black-throated divers, which are smaller cousins of the great northern diver, do, however, nest in Scotland, and the previous day, on a visit to Loch Shiel, I glimpsed a black-throated diver out on the water. They are handsome birds, with their grey heads, and sharply defined black throats bordered with wavy, dark, finely scribbled streaks. An endearing Scottish name for the black-throated diver is the northern doucker, a reference to its diving habits.

Loch Shiel was once home to the wildlife writer, Mike Tomkies, who lived in a remote cottage he called *Wildernesse*, where access on its hard-to-reach northern shore was only possible by a tough trek across rough ground or by boat. Previously a successful Fleet Street journalist and a

Hollywood columnist, he forsook fame and financial rewards to live in the wilds of Canada, and then, more latterly, the west Highlands of Scotland, to attain a closer insight into the wildlife found in such remote areas, including golden eagles, pine martens and red deer.

In his book, *Last Wild Years* (1992), Tomkies gained a unique insight into the black-throated divers of Loch Shiel, and even filmed a female in the process of laying an egg. He also recounted an intimate encounter with her mate when she was incubating on the nest:

> *Often she dozed, her eyelids closing from below. After a time the other diver came to the shore (the one I guessed was the male) and made 'oom' sounds. He kept tilting up his beak as he made these calls, as if saying 'come on, come out here'. Eventually the female gave in to his wishes and propelled herself down to join him in the sunny waters. I could see them through the bushes and little trees beside the hide – preening, showing their creamy bellies and the male presenting his mate with a small fish.*

It is wonderful writing and testimony to the dedication of a man where nature had become an all-consuming passion and his determination to ensure his experiences would aid the conservation of under-pressure species and the wider environment.

For my visit to Loch Shiel, I had taken the well-maintained track from Polloch on the south-western shore near Strontian, and shortly after seeing the diver, I gazed across the water to the cottage where Tomkies once lived. I scanned the hill ridges above in the hope of spotting a golden eagle, but the sky remained tantalisingly empty.

Loch Shiel is a long sliver of freshwater that stretches for 28 km from Acharacle in the south west to the famous Glenfinnan Monument in the north-east, erected in 1815 in tribute to the Jacobite clansmen who fought and died in the cause of Bonnie Prince Charlie during the 1745 Rising. This was a place bustling with life, including willow warblers eagerly delivering their sweet songs and a pair of male blackcaps bickering among the branches of a straggly birch. A small pebbly beach was too tempting to resist, so I hunkered on a waterside boulder to have lunch, where the distant melancholy wails of a black-throated diver broke the air, probably from the same bird I had seen earlier. In local folklore, if black-throated divers lose their young, a mournful song can be heard on the loch. It was too early in the season for egg laying to have even begun, so this was certainly no lament, and instead was the call of a male seeking a mate. The diver's cry had a wondrous uplifting quality, almost as if all of nature was singing out from the silver-flecked ripples of the loch.

Later that week, I spent time at Kentra Bay in the north-east of the Ardnamurchan peninsula, which lies close to Acharacle. It is a shallow sea bay comprising mud and sand at low tide, and where grassy, salt marsh encroaches upon the near shore. The liquid, trilling calls of curlews filled the air and a pair of greenshanks waded by the edge of a muddy pool. The greenshanks were on migration, and I was hoping to become better acquainted with these grey-coloured waders later in my wildlife odyssey when I ventured to their breeding grounds on the wild moors and damp flushes of Sutherland.

I walked further along the track away from Kentra Bay and through a forestry plantation until reaching the beach at Camas an Lighe, or The Singing Sands as it popularly known. Apparently, when the wind blows, the sands make a 'singing' noise, made possible by the particular shape and size of the sand grains found here, as well as the silica content.

I perched on a rocky outcrop and strained my ears to detect even a whisper of a song. At first, there was nothing of any real musical intent, apart from the crash of the surf breaking against the shore. Then, a familiar cry broke over the stiff sea breeze – the plaintive call of a great northern diver from somewhere out upon the low-crested waves. The diver called once more before falling quiet, only for a pair of oystercatchers to chime their familiar ringing 'kleep, kleep' calls. The sands might have remained stubbornly silent but their supporting acts were in full flow, ensuring that this was a beach where the music would never die.

Chapter 12

MYSTICAL ROWANS AND PREGNANT SEALS

May 2021 – Skye

It was a landscape that stirred the emotions, a place where the signs of past human occupation dotted the grassy pasture that sloped gently down towards the sea overlooking Loch Slapin, near Elgol in Skye. There were several ruined stone cottages, each one with a story to tell of generations of families enduring a simple yet incredibly tough existence, eking out a living from the land and sea on the remote Strathaird peninsula that looks across to Sleat.

Children would have played on the ground where I was standing while their parents toiled and worked the poor soil of their run-rig field systems. It was a challenging existence and by the end of the 1700s many had sought new lives overseas in the New World. Those that stayed behind often endured harsh treatment from the landowners, and crofter rebellions took place across Skye. As an example, people living in Staffin in the north of Skye were in dispute throughout much of the 1800s with landowners because of rent rises, insecurity of tenure and the eviction of families from their land. The unrest was part of a wider movement of land rights struggles, which culminated in the Crofters' War (that began in the 1870s) and the founding of the Crofters' Party in 1885.

I had no way of knowing if such turmoil had occurred on the ground where I was now standing near Kirkibost. Tales of woe, bloodshed and treachery, which will remain untold until the end of time, could well have been lying here before my eyes, or alternatively, perhaps this settlement had a peaceful past. A map survey of 1877, sourced from the National Library of Scotland online archive, shows the settlement, which is marked as 'An Reidhean'. I am uncertain if that name refers to the gathering of crofts or to the geographical area. Whether the settlement was still occupied in 1877, I do not know, but what immediately struck me with my naturalist's eye, was that each croft-house had a lone rowan tree growing beside it or rooted within a crumbled wall. Rowans are long-lived, and because each house had its own single tree by the south facing end, these trees had almost certainly been around since the settlement was last occupied, rather than being the result of later natural re-seeding.

Rowan (Ruined Cottage, Skye)

The rowans here, like those in the churchyards, had been planted to ward off witches, which, in the past, was a common practice among dwellers in the Highlands. Even up until the twentieth century, rowan boughs were hung over farm buildings. In parts of Scotland, cutting down a rowan tree is still considered a harbinger of bad luck, especially when close to a house. It is a tree that has long been venerated, including by Celtic druids, for its healing and medicinal properties. In herbal medicine, extracts from rowan bark were used to help ease diarrhoea and nausea and a concoction from the ripe berries was utilised to treat sore throats. In the Middle Ages, the hard pale brown wood of the rowan made excellent bows, and was used for tool handles, bowls and general woodcraft. The rowan is a truly remarkable tree, steeped in the heart of humanity from the earliest of times.

In many ways, rowans are the epitome of Scotland, having a stoic grip and determination that enables them to find hold on the poorest and shallowest of soils, or in rock crevices. They can survive extreme icy blasts

91

of winter weather for weeks on end, and stand like lone sentinels in our uplands, their branches sculpted by the wind.

As well as their faith in the witch-deterrent abilities of rowans, I am certain that the people who once lived in this little corner of Skye would have appreciated rowans for their aesthetic qualities too. Rowans throw up the most incredible creamy-white blooms in spring that are a magnet for pollinating hill insects, signalling hope and vitality. In autumn, they hang heavy with glistening red berries, providing sustenance for birds and other creatures, while the leaves develop a dazzling reddish hue shortly before dropping. Even in the barest days of winter, the trunk of a rowan shimmers and shines in a reflective silvery beauty. Also called the mountain ash, the rowan is strong in spirit and character yet has a delicateness and fragility that is strangely compelling.

Strathaird is a seductive corner of Skye, and the area around Kilmarie with its open birch woodlands and abundant wildflowers is especially serene. Early purple orchids dotted open clearings, bringing enchanting splashes of colour. All orchids have an inherent irresistible allure, probably because the word orchid itself has almost reverential qualities, conjuring images in the mind of the world's many incredibly coloured and exotically shaped tropical species.

Early Purple Orchid

Orchids are strongly associated with beauty and rarity, and this is what excites, although these two qualities are not always the case in Scotland with some of our species being reasonably common, such as the heath spotted-orchid, and others being quite dowdy – such as the lesser twayblade and creeping lady's-tresses.

Orchids have enthralled humanity since at least the start of recorded history and have long been associated with love and fertility. A concoction using ground orchid tubers was frequently used as an aphrodisiac and the name orchid itself is derived from the Greek orkhis, meaning testicle because of the shape of the root. The Greek physician, Dioscorides, believed that orchids influenced sexuality and that eating their roots could determine the sex of unborn children. Until recently, in Ireland and the Shetland Isles, orchids were used in love potions.

On the nearby John Muir Trust managed land at Strathaird, two other fascinating plants abounded – sundews and butterworts. It was a faint reddish tinge in a boggy margin that first drew my attention to the sundews which were only just emerging as the warmth of spring took hold. They are engaging little plants that are easily overlooked but behind their rather benign appearance lies a deadly killer, for like the better-known Venus flytrap, the sundew is carnivorous and feeds voraciously upon insects.

It is worthwhile to get down close and examine sundews more carefully, because close examination reveals in intricate detail their waxy leaves, coated in a forest of little red hairs, each one tipped with a tiny glistening droplet. These droplets are the deadly lure, the bait for the trap. The droplets are irresistibly attractive to a midge or other small insect and once the midge alights on the leaf it is trapped by sticky glands and slowly digested by a cocktail of enzymes. During this whole grisly process, the leaf edge gradually curls inwards to enclose the prey, much in the same manner as a clenched fist.

An upland bog is not the friendliest of places for a plant. The lack of nutrients is a particular problem which is why the sundew has evolved insect-catching as an innovative way of gaining valuable nourishment on such barren and waterlogged ground. The sundew is so-named because the tiny droplets on the leaves resemble dewdrops that appear every morning. The plant can be likened to a natural form of highly efficient flypaper, with one study estimating that sundews in a two-acre sized bog can trap about six million insects during a season. When one thinks of the abundance of midges in this part of Scotland, then the sundews have found a convenient source of nutrition and an important ecological niche.

The sundew has been used as a medicinal herb since the twelfth century and was considered a good remedy for whooping cough. The 'dew' was much treasured in medieval times for its claimed abilities for destroying warts, and rather bizarrely, female cattle were said to become sexually aroused by eating even a small quantity of the plant.

Butterworts were also common on the hill ground at Strathaird. The neat star-shaped rosette of yellow-green leaves entrap invertebrates on their sticky surfaces before being digested. The flower of the butterwort is more obvious than the sundew, being a beautiful violet colour and held aloft on a long nodding stem growing out from the centre of the rosette.

I walked further up the John Muir Trust path that eventually leads to Sligachan on the far side of the island. On reaching the brow of a hill, a magnificent vista unveiled itself to the south and south-west, including the islands of Eigg, Muck, Rum, Canna and Soay, which holds the remnants of on old basking shark hunting station set up by Gavin Maxwell, the author of *Ring of Bright Water* (1960). Directly to the west across Loch Slavaig rose the imposing, jagged ridge and peaks of the Black Cuillin.

The following day, I embarked upon a boat trip across Loch Slavaig towards Coruisk. On the approach to the berthing site at Loch na Cuilce, an otter scampered across an exposed part of the shore, and on a rocky islet, a large group of harbour seals basked. Many of these seals were bloated with pregnancy and were on the verge of giving birth. Harbour seals are gentler in appearance than the commoner, larger, and more heavily built grey seal, with their inquisitive eyes set upon softly rounded faces. The seals were well used to the comings and goings of the tourist boat and barely raised an eyebrow as we passed close by. Seen up close, the harbour seals exhibited marvellously patterned bodies, an intricate marbling, with some animals dark in background colour, whilst others were grey or rusty brown.

Harbour Seal (Loch Slavaig)

Once ashore, it was only a short walk to Loch Coruisk, a most striking freshwater loch bounded by the imposing Cuillin mountains on every flank. It was a surreal place, more rock than soil and grass, and with the aura of a completely different world, which inspired writers and artists such as Walter Scott and J M W Turner. Even where the Coruisk River entered the sea, the strength and power of the underlying rock predominated, with the water tumbling over large grey slabs without having made any significant impact of erosion over the millennia.

Grey, wispy clouds swirled around the highest peaks and a sudden shiver rippled down my spine. In that instance, I immediately understood why humanity in previous centuries would have so desperately sought solace from rowan trees as a form of protection from witches and other evils. In the past, this was a wild land where the power of nature reigned supreme and sparked fear and trepidation into the hearts of every living soul.

Chapter 13

A CLAMOURING SEABIRD CITY

May 2021 – Fowlsheugh, Aberdeenshire

It is hard to imagine a more absorbing scene of nature's overwhelming urge to procreate than the one I observed from the top of the towering seabird cliffs at Fowlsheugh, south of Stonehaven in Aberdeenshire. There were thousands of dramas being played out: guillemots courting, razorbills bickering and gulls patrolling for unguarded eggs to snatch.

Fowlsheugh embodies nature's wild soul, and the noise of the swirling seabirds, the heavy aroma of guano and the sight of thousands of bobbing birds out on the water was totally addictive. This is a seabird city, a place of life and death, and one where one becomes awed and bewildered in equal measure by its sheer vibrancy and clamour.

I adore Fowlsheugh, a wild sanctuary of contemplation, and my heart swells with tumultuous emotion on each visit, an uncontrollable heaving that leaves my mind spinning. Tens of thousands of guillemots, razorbills, kittiwakes and other seabirds nest here, a pulsating mass of frenetic life. Every dark bird dot on the cliff ledges represents a unique individual, each one with their own remarkable stories to tell – of survival and long oceanic wanderings, and near brushes with death. This was a coming together, a once-a-year opportunity to socialise with their kind, and the seabirds were clearly revelling in the joyous reunion.

Fowlsheugh means 'bird cliff'. It is one of the largest and most spectacular seabird colonies on mainland Britain. Three kilometres of red sandstone cliffs rise to over 60 m, with weathering having created crevices and ledges, which are ideal nesting sites for seabirds. The pink blooms of thrift and red campion sparkle along the clifftops and linnets bound along the edges of encroaching fields.

As ever, on my first arrival at this RSPB reserve, it was hard to decide where to look, such was the abundance of activity from every side. A constant stream of kittiwakes swooped low over the clifftops to settle on a grassy slope where they eagerly collected nesting material. Once their yellow beaks were full and brimming, they spiralled down below the cliff edge, using eddies from the swirling air currents to propel them towards their nesting ledges.

Other kittiwakes streamed along the clifftops on white-flashed wings, excitedly tumbling from side-to-side before spiralling down to the sea and then flying back from whence they came like a rolling avian conveyor belt. It appeared as if the kittiwakes were doing this for fun and sheer joy, and their excitement was palpable. Anthropomorphism – apportioning human characteristics to animals – is frowned upon among some, but the more I observe wildlife, the more I am convinced that emotions – such as joy and sadness – are one of the bedrocks of the animal kingdom. Think of the pleasure of a sunbathing blackbird on a garden lawn with wings spread open, or the cries of despair of a fox cub that has lost its mother. Animals are no different from us, we are as one.

Kittiwakes are elegant little gulls, intricate in form, graceful in flight and bundles of perfection. Yet they are among the toughest creatures around, spending most of the year out at sea in search of small surface-swimming fish or planktonic animals, venturing as far as Greenland and eastern Canada in their wanderings. The storms these birds must have endured over tumultuous seas are unimaginable, blown like wind-blasted and fragile fragments over the tempestuous, bitter cold ocean, where food must be all but impossible to find at times.

The emotion of life was reflected by one pair of kittiwakes on a rock ledge below where I stood, who canoodled up to one another, strengthening their bonds prior to egg laying and the start of incubation. Normally, kittiwakes would have been on eggs by now, but the unusually cold spring had probably delayed things by a week or two.

Nearby, a group of guillemots were courting, their heads bobbling up and down whilst other couples gently nibbled one another with their long, dagger-like beaks. Such harmonious scenes were precarious and spats would frequently break out between rival males or females who were not yet ready to relent to the continuous amorous attentions unleashed upon them.

A sloping rock shelf halfway down one section of cliff thronged with guillemots, their bodies tightly packed like sardines. These birds were a direct reflection of the sea's bounty, having spent the previous autumn and winter fishing its depths. It is a challenging and difficult maritime existence, and many guillemots succumb to fierce storms, their bodies washed ashore in huge rafts.

On another rock ledge lay the turquoise, pear-shaped egg of a guillemot, dangerously exposed and likely to be swooped upon by gulls at any time. There is the long-held belief that a guillemot egg is shaped this way, so that when accidently nudged, it rotates on its pointy end in an arc, thus preventing it rolling off the edge. New research, however, has revealed it is more likely that the eggs are pear-shaped because they are more stable on sloping rock ledges where the birds often nest. Such a design also brings strength. Guillemots often crash land onto their nests, especially on windy days, and the egg needs to be robust to prevent it getting crushed. There is a hygiene advantage too, with the blunt end sticking upwards clear of seabird muck, thus enabling the porous shell to breathe more easily.

Guillemots (Fowlsheugh)

Guillemots are steeped in folklore. They have a host of common names including frowl, marrot, murre, quet and sea hen. Such familiarity with humanity was no doubt due to their importance as a source of food in remote coastal and island communities, such as St Kilda. Their eggs were often collected but they were something of an acquired taste. Writing in the early twentieth century, the Reverend Neil Mackenzie noted that while 'they can be good eating when fresh' other eggs 'are as bad as the most vivid imagination can depict' ('Notes of the Birds of St Kilda', *Annals of Scottish Natural History* (1905)).

Razorbills were present, too, at Fowlsheugh, but in much smaller numbers than the guillemots and were less sociable, tending to group in pairs and sometimes rattling their bills with one another. Their distinctive serrated and laterally compressed bill is perfectly designed for gripping onto sandeels and butterfish.

Razorbill (Fowlsheugh)

Guillemots and razorbills are absorbing to watch, especially in early spring, when they first gather on cliff ledges or on the sea. They skid along the sea surface and there is much diving and chasing underwater. They also wheel in the air before swooping down to the sea like fearless daredevils. As the season progresses, boisterous accumulations of adults bob in the water, relishing the relaxation from the chores of incubating eggs or tending young.

Fulmars were incubating eggs on some of the grassier, broader ledges near the clifftops. Although the fulmar looks like a gull, it is in fact a petrel and is related to the albatross. Its bill is quite different from that of a gull and consists of a complicated arrangement of horny plates with a tubular nasal protuberance. Another characteristic of the fulmar is its stiff-winged gliding flight. Fulmars like nothing better than to wheel in the air currents with hardly a beat of the wings.

Being spewed upon by a fulmar is one of my more memorable, albeit unenjoyable, wildlife experiences. It happened a long time ago when I was ringing young gannets on the Bass Rock. Keen to take a photograph of a fulmar, I approached too close to one and it duly projectile-vomited a foul concoction of fishy oil over my jacket. It is a rather unsavoury defensive ploy adopted by fulmars to deter predators and I can certainly vouch for its effectiveness.

The old Viking word for fulmar means 'foul-gull' and these birds have long had a reputation for this unorthodox way of protecting their nests. Indeed, it is thought that an attempt to reintroduce four sea eagles to Fair Isle in 1968 may have failed partly because of fulmars. The eagles began to prey upon the fulmars, who in turn were quick to hit back with their deadly deterrent. Ornithologists soon found a male eagle with matted feathers that was heavily soiled in fulmar oil. It died a few weeks later.

Fulmar (Fowlsheugh)

Fulmars feed on a variety of oceanic foods ranging from zooplankton to offal and discards from commercial fishing vessels. With Scotland's fishing fleets now having moved to a new discard-free catching regime, it will be interesting to see what impact this has on fulmar and other seabird populations.

Prior to the mid-nineteenth century, the Scottish fulmar population was confined mainly to St Kilda, but they have shown a remarkable range of expansion since, which mirrored the rise in commercial fishing, and they are now common around our coasts.

Like the kittiwake, fulmars are great wanderers, spreading their wings far and wide in their quest for the ocean's riches. As with other seabirds, fulmars face great challenges: climate change impacting upon food availability and the ever-present threat of inadvertently ingesting marine plastic. Fulmars can live up to 40 years and any impact such environmental factors may have on their numbers could take time to detect. My impression, however, on this visit was that there were fewer nesting fulmars at Fowlsheugh than a decade ago.

On the far side of the reserve is a steep grassy slope by a sea cave where puffins often nest, but despite persistent scanning with my binoculars, I could not find any that time around. They are scarce birds in mainland Scotland, preferring to nest on islands, such as the Isle of May at the mouth of the Firth of Forth where their nesting burrows are safe from rats and other ground predators such as weasels and stoats.

As I made my way back along the clifftop, I found a small mound of black feathers. This was the remains of a jackdaw that had been plucked out of the sky by a marauding peregrine falcon. The cliffs can provide plentiful pickings for a pair of peregrines, a rich larder from which to raise their own family. Rock doves would be another regular staple for peregrines at Fowlsheugh, although adult guillemots and razorbills would probably be a step too far, given their size and feisty nature.

Near the pile of jackdaw feathers was a grassy hummock which provided a good vantage point on which to sit and gaze out over the North Sea and appreciate the abundance of seabirds tumbling above the cliffs. As the air heaved and reverberated from the clamouring calls of the ocean, I wondered what the future held for these birds. They are the pearls of the ocean, so special, yet so vulnerable, especially from the impact of climate change.

There was also a missing cousin of the guillemots and razorbills to reflect upon. Many centuries ago, at Fowlsheugh, on gentler slopes below the teeming throngs of cliff nesters, there would in all probability have been great auks too. Archaeological evidence suggests that in the distant past this large flightless auk was tolerably common in some coastal parts of Scotland. Unfortunately, they were relentlessly hunted, and the last Scottish great auk was killed by trophy collectors in Orkney in 1813. A few decades later, the only remaining pair in the world met a similar fate in

Iceland, a telling reminder of the fragility of nature and the devastation so often wrought by the hand of man.

Fowlsheugh and its abundant bird-life is a tangible indicator of the importance of our oceans and seas. It reminds us of the need for eradicating pollution and ensuring fisheries are well managed and sustainable, along with maintaining an ambitious programme of Marine Protected Areas to protect the most vulnerable species and underwater habitats. The sea is everything in our environment; it is the driving force that supports so much else.

Plastic is a particular modern-day problem, and shortly before starting my Scottish wildlife odyssey, I came upon an atrocity of such debris on a remote Skye beach. The plastic was all around, an abomination that struck at the heart of the respect we should have for our planet, a proliferation of plastic bottles, cartons, fishing net fragments and the like. A wave of anger engulfed me. What are we doing to our precious planet and how soon are we going to act before we destroy it forever?

Recent studies have revealed that every single seal, whale and dolphin washed up on British shores had traces of plastic in its stomach, as did every fulmar. Plastic is ingested by fish and shellfish and has even been discovered in our deepest living marine organisms. It is everywhere, an omnipresent threat that is choking the lifeblood out of our precious marine environment, and with that, threatening humanity too. With such dark thoughts racing through my mind, I rose from my seat by the plucked jackdaw feathers and slowly headed back to my starting point at the small settlement of Crawton.

Chapter 14

BOTTLENOSE DOLPHINS AND
SCREECHING TERNS

May 2021 – Aberdeen and the Ythan Estuary

I came more out of hope than expectation, and on initially scanning the sea off the mouth of Aberdeen Harbour, it was strangely devoid of life. There was only a small group of cormorants resting on the southern breakwater and a handful of herring gulls wheeling in the sky.

I am used to such inauspicious starts when searching for wildlife, and was in no mood to concede, because this small car park by the fortified ancient monument of the Torry Battery is one of the best places in Scotland to observe bottlenose dolphins. The search would need to be intensified so I descended some steps towards the shore of the outer harbour basin. Halfway down, I paused and swept the sea once more with binoculars. For May, it was bitterly cold with a northerly breeze and blustery rain showers swirling intermittently in from the steely North Sea. My fingers quickly became numb.

Every dark wave-crest momentarily sparked an imaginary vision of a rolling dolphin fin, only for the tumbling shadowy peak of the surge to dissipate into grey ocean once more. The undulating sea was playing tricks on the mind. It is so much easier spotting dolphins when the water is placid and calm. I persevered and looked once more, and this time a dark fin and an arched back perceptibly broke the water, and then did so again. This was no dreamy vision, but an actual dolphin, which briefly surfaced several times more. It was quite far offshore, gambolling in the water close to an anchored offshore oil-support vessel. Further scrutiny with my binoculars soon revealed several other dolphins, which were swimming either in pairs or singly, rather than as one large group.

The mouth of Aberdeen Harbour, where the River Dee spills out into the sea, is attractive to dolphins because of migrating salmon and sea trout funnelling into the port entrance. Smolts – which are young salmon leaving the river in April and May to embark upon their oceanic wanderings

– are also eagerly devoured. Dolphins are found off the harbour all year round, although the best months to spot them are April, May, June and July, and it is not unusual for bottlenose dolphins to feed and play close to the two breakwaters. On one occasion several years ago I watched in almost disbelief as dolphins rolled and dived within the confines of the harbour. Here, by the edge of one of Scotland's principal cities were wild dolphins, finding a good living and completely nonplussed by the constant coming and goings of oil-support ships, often jumping and riding in their bow waves for a bit of fun. It was enthralling to watch them tumbling in the water, and now, whenever I visit Aberdeen, the harbour mouth is where I am drawn to first.

Bottlenose Dolphin (Aberdeen Harbour)

Rather than feeding, the bottlenoses I had just encountered were probably lingering offshore to wait for the optimum tidal conditions which would encourage salmon to start moving into the Dee (or exiting the river in the case of smolts), at which time they would move in closer to the harbour entrance. As such, the presence of dolphins is not always immediately obvious to casual observers and using binoculars and regularly scanning the sea offshore will dramatically increase the chances of detecting them.

The dolphins here are part of the famous Moray Firth population, which are mobile in their behaviour, venturing far and wide down the east coast of Scotland as far as Berwickshire and sometimes beyond. Indeed, one of my most memorable dolphin encounters was when walking with my family several years ago along the coastal path to the south east of St Andrews \\\\\\\\\\\\\\\\\\\\\\\\\\\\\'/\ we spotted a large pod of bottlenoses close to the shore. The sea was enveloped in rolling mist, but as the sun began to burn off the grey, ethereal murk, the dolphins suddenly materialised, some leaping spectacularly clear of the water. It was a wonderful sight that was accompanied by shouts of excitement from our two children. As the dolphins moved across the bay it was even possible to see some animals breaching clear of the sea against the backdrop of the spires and buildings of St Andrews.

It is estimated that there are around 200 bottlenose dolphins in eastern Scotland, with a further 50 or so resident on the west coast around the Hebrides. Researchers can estimate the size of the population reasonably accurately by using photo identification techniques that can differentiate between the unique nicks and notches on the fins of individuals. Dolphins are long-lived animals and have only been studied in recent times, which makes it difficult to determine any long-term trends in numbers, but indications suggest that the eastern Scottish population is probably stable. Scotland holds the most northerly resident populations of bottlenose dolphins in the world, and we have a tremendous responsibility to look after them.

Interestingly, historical literature provides little tangible evidence of the occurrence of bottlenose dolphins in Scottish waters in the more distant past. Whether this is because they were absent, or is simply down to the lack of observer records or the animals being classed as porpoises, is unclear. A report published by Scottish Natural Heritage in 2011 ('Distribution, Abundance and Population Structure of Bottlenose Dolphins in Scottish Waters') found historical records to be sparse, even from today's core population area of the Moray Firth. Thomas Edward, a naturalist who lived in Banff in the mid-nineteenth century, recorded four cetacean species from the area, including the bottlenose dolphin. While harbour porpoises were described as 'frequently seen', Edward merely stated that the bottlenose dolphin 'is said to have been taken here, though there are doubts as to the fact'. It is entirely possible, therefore, that it is only in more recent times that bottlenose dolphins have become established in Scottish waters.

Harbour Porpoise

I studied zoology at the University of Aberdeen and lived in the city for 14 years, making it a place of tremendous affinity that is ingrained in my being. One of my regular haunts at the time was Aberdeen's other estuary, the Don, which bounds the northern side of the city. Thus, buoyed by my dolphin encounter by the Dee, I ventured up to the Don, taking the path from Seaton Park to the Brig o' Balgownie and down to the mouth of the estuary where a pair of goosanders bobbed out on the water. The rest of the estuary was otherwise quiet, with most waders and waterfowl having departed to their northern breeding grounds. The bracing, briny air was invigorating and while nature was lying low, the familiarity of the estuary was like a soothing comfort blanket, and it felt good to be back within its wild hold.

Estuaries are special places, brimming with life, and there is no better example in Scotland than the Ythan Estuary, several kilometres further north of the mouth of the River Don, which was my final port of call. A visit to the estuary and the surrounding Forvie National Nature Reserve at any time of year is engrossing. In May one can expect to see curlews and shelducks feeding on the muddy shore, whilst out in the river channel the air rings to the final, end-of-season crooning calls of courting eiders. Most of the female eiders on the Ythan were sitting on eggs, hidden among the sand-dunes, and the few remaining ones out on the water were continually being pestered by drakes, desperate for the last opportunity to mate before the breeding season's end. Eiders feed largely upon mussels which are abundant in the Ythan. They swallow them whole with their powerful gizzards, crushing them into highly nutritious food. Forvie National Nature Reserve is managed by ScotNature and boasts one of Britain's highest breeding concentrations of eiders. It is one of the largest expanses of sand-dunes in Scotland and also includes significant areas of maritime heath. As the sands shift with the breeze and the tides, different habitats are created, ensuring a rich and dynamic environment. Dips and hollows in among the dunes, or slacks as they are known, can be dry or damp depending upon the level of the water table, each type holding their own different range of flora and insects, including northern marsh orchids and crowberries, and dark green fritillary and grayling butterflies.

Marram grass is one of the predominant plants on the shifting dunes, a natural anchor, where the fibrous and convoluted root system provides a degree of stability to the infirmity of the sand. This grey-green, prickly grass is a pioneer species, and its fragile tenure provides the path for other plants and creatures to colonise the dunes. Marram is superbly well adapted to this harsh, wind-blown environment where the free-draining sand is bereft of moisture – the plant's waxy leaves roll intricately inwards to prevent evaporation from the surface.

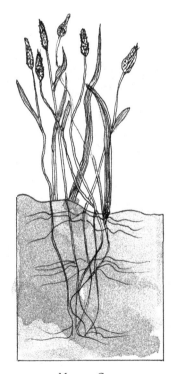

Estuaries, such as the Ythan, are nourished and fuelled by an alternating two-way flow of nutrients from the sea and land that makes a typical estuary hugely productive and incredibly rich in invertebrate life. The productivity figures are astonishing, and studies in the Ythan estuary have revealed that a square metre of mud is home to a multitude of minute shrimps, mud snails, ragworms and tiny clams. There can be few, if any, other environments in the world that can match such richness.

Marram Grass

Standing by the margin of the estuary near Newburgh brought vivid recollections of sampling the gloopy mud for invertebrates as part of my university course. I was a wayward student and not in the least studious, which is something I regret, and as I reflected upon opportunities missed, a large bird glided across the sky and started to hover above the river. My first inclination was that it was a great black-backed gull, but I quickly realised it was an osprey, methodically covering the estuary in search of sea trout and flounders. It floated above a fly-fisher who had waded out deep into the river, man and bird engaged in the same quest for fish, before slowly making its way to the mouth of the estuary, intermittently hovering on large, floppy wings.

Glimpsing an osprey over the Ythan would have been unthinkable in my university days in the 1980s, and the presence of the bird represented a remarkable reminder of the many strides that have been made in nature conservation over the past few decades. It is easy to become gloomy and despondent about the prospects for nature, but there are numerous positive stories of flora and fauna prospering once more after years of decline or local extinction. This is something that should never be forgotten and represents a beacon of hope and opportunity.

I followed the north shore of the estuary until reaching a fenced-off area where further access was not permitted because of a vulnerable ground-nesting colony of sandwich, Arctic, common and little terns. I could see the birds in the distance through my binoculars, wheeling excitedly and chasing each other in swooping flocks, their shrieking cries filling the air in a whirlwind of piercing noise.

Terns are fickle by nature, and breeding numbers can fluctuate greatly in any one place over time, some years being abundant, and in others scarce or even absent. The sandwich terns nesting by the Ythan have been doing well in recent times, and on my visit numbered a little over 1,000 pairs, while there were around 1,000 pairs of Arctic terns and 100 pairs of common terns. The rarest is the dainty little tern, with only about 20 pairs currently nesting.

The rich nutrients from tern droppings encourages a prolific growth of vegetation, including nettles, which seems to benefit nesting black-headed gulls. The ternery is protected by electric fencing to deter predators such as foxes and badgers, and without such intervention, successful nesting would not be possible.

Sandwich Terns (Ythan Estuary)

On my return journey, a movement on the path paused my progress – a small, black and orange hairy caterpillar, topped with a fringe of grey, was moving incredibly fast along the ground in rippling undulations. It was the caterpillar of a garden tiger moth, sometimes known as a 'woolly bear'. In a couple of months, this intriguing hairy creature will transform into an intricately-patterned moth, its brown, white and red wings flashing over the dunes on warm, calm nights. The wind-scoured dunes and heaths of Forvie might at first glance appear inhospitable, but within its bounds, life thrives and prospers, a testament to nature's ability to evolve and adapt, no matter the challenges of the environment.

Chapter 15

A PERFECT DAY IN THE BRAEMAR HILLS

June 2021 – The Cairngorms

It was the perfect beginning to what turned out to be a perfect day – a dawn start at Inverey, near Braemar, and with each passing step, an abundance of wildlife revealed itself on my trek up Glen Ey, which lies in the southern Cairngorms, including curlews, green hairstreak butterflies and a dazzling array of wildflowers.

Glen Ey has a special hold on my heart. It is the place I first ventured on hillwalking trips as a teenager when accompanied by school friends, and where I return to most years, drawn by its warm embrace. I recall the thrill and excitement of finding my first ever breeding dotterels on the surrounding mountain plateaux and watching golden eagles soaring high in the sky on wide-splayed wings. For an impressionable teenager, the excitement of seeing these birds in the flesh was overwhelming, as, before then, they had only shone out as illustrations in bird identification books.

Golden Eagle (GlenEy)

It was wonderful to return to Glen Ey once more and as I embarked upon my venture that dawn morning it felt like a homecoming. I drew immense wellbeing from the familiarity of the hills and the verdant meadows of the glen floor. Not long after leaving the attractive hamlet of

Inverey, a group of stags materialised on a heathery knoll, standing proud and their antlers in full velvet. They were not shy and enabled me to approach reasonably close. One of the stags sported magnificent, multi-pronged antlers, a true 'Monarch of the Glen'. It was strange how these stags were so content in one another's company, when in only a few months' time they will become mortal foes as they compete for the attention of hinds during the annual rut. Such contrast underlines the importance of body chemistry in everyday animal behaviour, with a surge of testosterone in the autumn causing these seemingly benign stags to turn into sex-obsessed creatures, determined to fight their corner against other stags and mate with as many hinds as possible.

Red Deer Stag (Glen Ey)

The rut, which lasts from late September to early November, is a dramatic time in the Scottish hills. One of my most memorable experiences of the occasion was in Glen Mark in Angus several years ago, when after careful stalking, I managed to approach close to a harem of hinds that a master stag had rounded up for himself. From my hidden vantage point, I could clearly discern the stag with his heavy and impressive antlers bowing his head and letting rip a deep-throated bellow, before rushing at another stag that was edging upon his small harem of hinds. The message was unequivocal: 'keep off, these females are mine.'

111

It was a tiresome task, and as soon as the stag countered one male interloper, another would gradually encroach upon the other side of the harem, causing the stag to rush back again in anger and snort his defiance. When trying to defend a harem, it is nigh on impossible for the master stag to keep an eye on all of them all the time. This has resulted in the development of different mating strategies with some of the younger and less dominant males waiting for the opportunity to quickly rush in and mate with a hind when the attention of the harem master is otherwise engaged. One of my zoology lecturers at Aberdeen University dubbed these hit-and-run stags as 'sneaky copulators'.

All that sexual drama still lay several months away and the stags I was observing in Glen Ey were the picture of calm contentment. Across on the other side of the glen, a large herd of hinds had also congregated. They would soon be calving, dropping their young in the thick heather, where in their early days of life they are vulnerable to golden eagles. Outside the breeding season, stags and hinds generally do not mix, preferring to keep the company of their own gender.

On watching the peacefully-grazing hinds through my binoculars I pondered why red deer management has become such a controversial and complex issue. Where the populations are too high, their presence can be damaging to the environment, most notably through overgrazing and the prevention of the natural regeneration of trees. Red deer, however, are native to our shores and a vital part of the landscape, with deer carrion being an important source of food for a variety of upland wildlife, especially golden eagles. Red deer are also important economically, creating the direct employment associated with their management, along with a variety of downstream activities that contribute to rural employment. As ever, the crux of these difficult management issues is one of our own making and it is all about achieving the right balance. Red deer are essentially forest animals, but humanity over the centuries has felled the majority of natural forest cover, resulting in many deer adapting to life on the open hill. Furthermore, the eradication of the wolf and lynx has removed keystone predators, thus leaving numbers to spiral out of control unless there is management intervention.

It was tempting to linger with this herd of hinds in Glen Ey for a while longer as they were such attractive beasts, but my intention was to climb

Beinn Iutharn Mhòr, a large brooding mountain that stands at the top of glen, so I moved on. Further up the glen, several curlews wheeled about in the air, their liquid and haunting trilling calls whirling across the breeze. Sadly, curlew numbers are dwindling across the country, but here in Glen Ey they were prospering, with the mix of herb-rich grassland and damp flushes suiting their needs perfectly.

A lapwing spiralled in the sky above me on broad floppy wings, its high-pitched and repetitive 'pee-wee' call a warning that it had chicks nearby and that I should move away. The bird made several low passes, sometimes swooping so close I could hear the thrum of its wings.

A hearty song quickly drew my attention away from the spiralling lapwing: a melodic, ringing whistle which reflected the wildness of the landscape. It was a cock ring ouzel in full flow, singing from atop a boulder on the lower part of a slope. The ring ouzel is sometimes known as the mountain blackbird, and it is indeed like a blackbird, with the principal physical differences being a startling white crescent across the breast, and silvery-grey wing flashes. I first became acquainted with ring ouzels as a teenager when roaming the Pentland and Moorfoot Hills to the south of Edinburgh, where they were reasonably common at that time in steep-sided valleys and glens. Unfortunately, all that has changed and the ring ouzel has been declining for decades and is much scarcer, resulting in it now being red-listed as a bird of high conservation concern.

Ring ouzels are migratory, spending the winter in northern Africa and arriving back in Scotland in early spring. In nearby Glen Clunie, they have been intensively studied by researchers, and it is thought that a combination of factors is driving the fall in numbers, principally linked to a reduction in suitable habitat on their breeding and wintering grounds, as well as migration routes. It is a story repeated *ad nauseum* throughout nature – if the favoured habitat for one species becomes degraded or destroyed, the fortunes of a host of other animals and plants are also adversely affected because of their interdependence on one another and the ecosystem tumbles like a house of cards.

A long-eared head popped up above a knoll on the other side of the Ey Burn, the watercourse that runs down the middle of Glen Ey, and which is more a small river than a burn. It was a mountain hare, which watched me warily. Individual mountain hares have different personalities, some are confiding and sit tight, others are skittish and flee at the slightest hint of danger. This one was in the latter camp, and despite being a reasonable distance away, it was concerned by my presence, and lolloped away under the power of its incredibly long hind legs.

Mountain Hare (Glen Ey)

Mountain hares are attractive animals and this one looked magnificent in its smoky-blue summer coat. In a few months' time when winter takes hold, their fur will moult to white, providing seamless camouflage in the snowy expanses of the Cairngorms. If red deer are controversial, so too are mountain hares, which is perplexing, for they are such beautiful and harmless creatures. Until the recent past, large numbers of mountain hares were shot annually by grouse moor managers on the grounds they carry ticks and diseases such as louping-ill virus, which they supposedly spread to red grouse, and because they may damage tree saplings through their grazing.

As is the case with red deer, I would never oppose sensible management if required, but to me, the past culling of mountain hares was no more than mindless mass slaughter of one of Scotland's iconic animals, for they are part of the soul of the mountain environment. Fortunately, the outcry from the culling resulted in the implementation of recent legislation by the Scottish Government that gives mountain hares greater protection, so that it is now illegal to intentionally kill, injure or take mountain hares at any time unless a licence is obtained. While this is not total protection, it is certainly a step in the right direction, and it seems likely that the activity of killing mountain hares to control tick populations will not be licensable, given the lack of evidence that it is an effective form of tick management.

This is a thorny issue and licences to cull are most likely to be issued to prevent damage being caused to tree saplings or sensitive habitats through grazing. That is fine in as far as it goes, however, the mountain hare is different, for unlike red deer, it still has many natural predators, including foxes, golden and sea eagles, and stoats predating upon youngsters, which is a much better way of controlling numbers. A healthy environment needs a natural balance between predators and prey, not an unnatural one controlled solely by the hand of humanity.

I soon threw such thoughts aside to ponder upon another day, for as I continued up Glen Ey, the ground beneath my feet erupted into a legion of wildflowers, including the delicate yellow blooms of tormentil and blousy pink-petalled lousewort. A drift of mountain pansies also brightened a small incline by a slow-running tributary burn. They are among our most stunning wildflowers – little purple gems of perfection, with their two large top petals looking somewhat akin to rabbit ears. In the centre of the flower is a glowing heart of sunshine, gently inscribed with darker lines, which are 'honey guides' to help lure insects into the centre of the bloom.

Glen Ey is a classic U-shaped glen, the result of glaciation scouring a deep-sided and flat-bottomed valley, where there are hummock-like moraines, kettle holes and huge boulders dropped randomly by the ice as it melted. I paused for a while, sitting on a flat-topped boulder and gazed at the panorama before me. It was challenging to conjure in the mind what this landscape would have looked like in the Ice Age, covered in an impenetrable frozen hold that held such power it was able to carve into the bedrock like a knife through butter. The strength of glaciers verges on the unimaginable and their erosive action and depositional processes have sculpted and moulded Scotland into the land of today.

The symmetry of the glen was striking with its steep flanks centred by a broad, grassy plain, where the Ey Burn meandered in lazy fashion. The vibrant greenness of the glen floor contrasted starkly with the darker heather on the surrounding slopes, where grey scree fields and sporadic rocky outcrops scattered the hill flanks and spurs. It was wonderful to see native tree planting having taken place along the Ey Burn, protected by deer fencing – an example of pragmatic land management delivering tangible benefit. These native birches, rowans and other trees will eventually provide stability to the banksides, and their overhanging branches will drip invertebrates into the Ey Burn, providing rich pickings for trout and salmon parr.

Suddenly, a large bird swooped along a hill flank before rising further into the air so that its large, rectangular wings silhouetted against the morning sky. I uttered an involuntary yelp of glee, for it was a golden eagle and the first one I has seen since the start of my Scottish wildlife odyssey back in March. In many ways it was a relief because I had expected to see golden eagles on earlier stages of my nature journey, such as in Skye and Appin, but the skies had remained tantalisingly empty. This one soared high above me before disappearing at great speed around a hill spur.

For many people, the golden eagle is their ideal of the supreme predator – all power and strength and thriving on a diet of large prey items such as red deer calves and mountain hares. While this is certainly true, the golden eagle can also hunt in the most undistinguished manner when the opportunity arises. I recall once coming across a male golden eagle in Glen Isla, in Angus, which had adopted the unorthodox technique of hunting on foot. The enterprising bird had found a colony of spawning frogs and was wading through the shallow boggy pools, gulping them down one after another. There is even a recorded instance of a pair of eagles who specialised in raiding the nests of little meadow pipits. The eagles would seek out the nest sites by watching the parent pipits bringing in food before swooping down to pluck the wee fledglings out.

At the other end of the scale, the distinguished naturalists and research scientists, Desmond Nethersole-Thompson and Adam Watson, in their classic book *The Cairngorms* (1981), recounted a sighting by J Oswald, the head keeper in Glen Tanar, near Aboyne in Deeside, who once watched a pair of eagles combine in a hunt for capercaillies on the estate's pine forest. One eagle flew low through the woods to flush the capers out whilst the other, soaring above, would try to pounce as soon as one of the lumbering birds had cleared the treetops.

On another occasion, Oswald saw an eagle dive-bombed a young roe deer. The first time it hit the fawn on the shoulder but the mother roe reared on her hind legs and lashed out. She did this five more times, each time forcing the eagle to veer away. Thus, from frogs and baby birds to capercaillies and roe deer, the golden eagle is indeed a most versatile predator.

One golden eagle pair I came to know well in the 1980s resided in a remote glen on the fringes of the Cairngorms. For several years, it had become a compulsive habit of mine to visit – in late December and early January – this lonely glen to check how *my* eagles were doing, such was my affinity with the pair. It may have only been the turn of the year, and the weather was often cold and snowy, yet already these birds were thinking about breeding.

From a vantage point high on a slope on the far side of the glen, and far enough away to avoid disturbance, I could scrutinise through my binoculars the distant eyrie perched on a small jutting crag. Occasionally, it was possible to discern the fresh greenery of pine needles from sticks recently placed by the birds, a clear sign that the first preparations for egg laying in March had begun in earnest.

The eagles only bred in this crag eyrie every second or third year, utilising another eyrie in a nearby Scots pine at other times and not breeding at all in some years, although it was possible they had another nest in the area I had not found. Such nest rotation is typical of golden eagles and they often have two or three eyries in their territory.

Golden eagle courtship is a spectacular affair, which includes an array of different aerial displays, including a hypnotic undulating flight and sometimes birds will even roll upside down with their legs extended. Jeff Watson, in his monograph *The Golden Eagle* (1997), recounted one fascinating instance where the male bird rose into the air carrying a small rock. He circled upwards and then dropped the rock, entered a steep dive and caught it before it struck the ground. This action was repeated before the female took to the air to join him, herself carrying a clod of earth that was dropped and caught in the same manner. Such behaviour may be a signal of the birds' prowess and skill in catching prey, and thus a useful indicator of mate suitability.

The early twentieth century Scottish naturalist, and golden eagle expert, Seton Gordon, wrote:

Most of the eagle's courtship is aerial, and consists of
superb aerobatics, both male and female taking an equal part.
The male may swing over the female with wings raised, or he
may stoop at and chase her.

Golden eagles are intriguing birds and there is still much to learn about their behaviour. I was thrilled with my Glen Ey sighting, despite the encounter being brief. Not long after, I reached Altanour Lodge, a ruined shooting lodge that is supposedly haunted and which is surrounded by an isolated plantation of larch. From there, I struck up the flank of the nearby Beinn Iutharn Mhòr where, in a dark peat hag, I stumbled upon the well-preserved roots of several ancient trees – a reminder that in times long past this was a forested landscape, rather than the open and largely treeless one of today. Further on in the ascent, a frog jumped out from the thick heather under my feet. I crouched down to examine it and was immediately struck by its striking brick-red colouration combined with darker spots and streaks. The mountains of Scotland are a stronghold for frogs due to the high rainfall and innumerable pools and ditches for spawning. Thick heather cover also provides the perfect shelter from soaring birds of prey, enabling frogs to venture far and wide in their foraging, and in an environment that is humid and protected from bright sunshine and strong winds.

The flora on the ascent continually drew my eye, especially the white blooms of cloudberry and a patch of dwarf cornel that gleamed in the sunshine. Dwarf cornel is an interesting plant. Its creamy white flowerheads are deceptive, because rather than being petals, they are bracts, which are upper leaves of the stem, with the actual bluish-black flowers being crammed in a compressed huddle in the centre.

As I gained height, the heather dwindled and the landscape became starker and more exposed, particularly so on the approach to the summit (at over 1,000m in height). Whereas minutes before, I had been in a tranquil and warm environment, now there was an icy breeze, which acted as herald to my arrival into what is effectively an arctic-alpine setting. The bare exposed rock and boulder fields were encrusted with lichens and mosses, and on the summit ridge, patches of purple-pink trailing azalea flowers shone out. It is a mountain specialist with exquisite little flowers that form a creeping mat across the ground. The leaves are waxy and are presumably designed to prevent desiccation in the searing winds that whip across these high tops.

I noticed a movement to my right so I paused. Nearby, a ptarmigan strutted cautiously across a mountain-top boulder field, its grey and white plumage blending in harmony with the rough, weather-hewn rocks. A member of the grouse family, the ptarmigan is a remarkable bird, its plumage changing with the seasons, merging and matching in sympathy with the surroundings. In winter, the ptarmigan is almost completely white; its spring and summer plumage is a cryptic mottled grey, brown and white. The feet of the bird are completely feathered, which not only prevents heat loss, but acts as a useful pair of snowshoes in winter. Crowberry is an important food plant and ptarmigan feast upon their glossy black fruits in late summer.

Ptarmigan (Beinn Iutharn Mòhr)

The ptarmigan is a relic of the last Ice Age and is one of our few birds that can be classed as a real specialist of the arctic-alpine zone. It is also a bird that is prone to give the unsuspecting hillwalker something approaching a heart attack, sitting tight and invisible until the last second before exploding airborne at the walker's feet in a clatter of wings. It also makes itself known to the dedicated Munro bagger in other ways. In the thick mist that shrouds the high tops so frequently, many hillwalkers will be familiar with the rather peculiar experience of the enveloping blanket of grey silence being broken by the hoarse croaking of ptarmigan. Is it one bird, or two or three? It is always hard to tell.

Ptarmigan are normally approachable birds, but this one on Beinn Iutharn Mhòr was unusually timid and soon took to the air, wheeling away into the distance on white-flashed wings. I had hoped to see dotterel, which are small plovers, but despite persistent searching, none materialised. Dotterels have been an obsession of mine ever since I had first encountered them as a teenager in the surrounding mountains, and for many years I would embark upon annual pilgrimages to these high tops to seek them out. Attractive, tame and confiding, it is easy to come under their beguiling spell.

Dotterel are specialists of high mountain plateaux above 800m, their strongholds lying in the Cairngorms and adjacent mountains. One of the most remarkable features of the dotterel is the unusual sexual role reversal where the male is largely responsible for parental care. The slightly larger and brighter plumaged female takes the lead in courtship and display. She may also have more than one mate and once she has laid her eggs will for the most part leave the male to get on with the chores of incubating and looking after the young. Indeed, such is the nature of the female that she may lay her first clutch of eggs in Scotland, before swooping off across the North Sea to the mountains of Norway in search of another mate.

Despite the absence of dotterel, the high-altitude air of Beinn Iutharn Mhòr was invigorating, and I felt enthused and ebullient in this exposed mountain environment with its inspiring views. To the north, the high Cairngorm massif was etched against the horizon, and I reeled off the names of their summits automatically in my head; such familiar tops and each one the source of happy memories from the past in search of eagles, dotterel, ptarmigan and snow buntings. To the south lay the nearby summits of Carn an Righ, Mam nan Carn and Beinn Iutharn Bheag, below which nestled Loch nan Eun. I have fond recollections of this loch, camping there many years ago, and I recall that it was brimming with brown trout, the circular ripples of their rises peppering the water on a calm summer's evening.

Ever since that visit to Loch nan Eun, these isolated mountain trout have intrigued me. How did they get there? Were they introduced, or like the ptarmigan, are they also remnants from the last Ice Age? And if so, presumably they are now genetically unique compared to other trout populations? I enjoy these natural conundrums, especially since the answers usually remain tantalisingly elusive.

On the descent from Beinn Iutharn Mhòr, I inadvertently flushed a cock red grouse, which trailed its wing along the ground, pretending to be injured. I have seen female birds use this clever ploy before as a ruse to lure a predator away from her eggs or chicks, but I had not realised male birds also utilised the technique. A mother grouse must be nearby, so I parted the heather with my hands, and there she was, frozen stock still. The way she had hunkered down indicated that newly-hatched chicks were sheltering beneath her belly, so I carefully placed the heather back, and slowly retreated, leaving the grouse and her brood in peace. It had been a perfect day in the Cairngorms, and this had proved the perfect ending.

Chapter 16

THE DRAMA OF THE WILDWOOD

June 2021 – Strathspey

Silence, total silence. Not a rustle of wind nor peep of birdsong, just an enveloping hush seeping into every pore of this wildwood in Strathspey. This is what the dawn of time must have felt like, a mystical place where wolves and bears once roamed and where a thousand stories remain untold.

I gazed with lazy eyes at the myriad of Scots pines stretching away into the vast expanse of Abernethy Forest, near Aviemore, the lower branches of the trees grey-dripped with old man's beard and other lichens. It had been a while since my last visit to Abernethy Forest and I breathed every ounce of the warm air as if it were my last.

Even in early summer, I find these ancient pine wildwoods serenely quiet places. There was scattered birdsong about: the soft warbling of a robin, the chirpy calls of

Scots Pine Cone

chaffinches and the thin seeps of coal tits, but for the most part the forest was muted. For a moment, I thought my eyesight was going hazy, for a breeze suddenly picked up, and the woodland became almost opaque in a green, wispy mist. The surface of a dark, peaty pool by the track edge was similarly coated with a powder-puff greenness. On looking closely, I realised it was pollen from the Scots pines, billowing across the woodland whenever the wind blew, a swirling mist of new life that would ensure the creation of future generations of trees.

A gentle trilling and my enquiring mind became alert once more to a new mystery, for this was a most unusual call. There it went again. I looked across towards the direction of the source and spotted a wee gem of a bird with a diminutive, speckled crest and white cheeks – a crested tit. They are one of the unique creatures of these northern forests. Crested tits are peculiar because they have no wanderlust whatsoever and have never spread to other central and southern parts of Scotland, despite there being suitable areas for them, especially in nearby Deeside. It seems that the mountainous expanse of the Cairngorms acts as a natural barrier they are unwilling to cross. They are real home birds, happy with their lot.

A few thousand years ago around a half to two-thirds of Scotland was wildwood but today only a handful of clusters remain, most notably the Caledonian pinewoods of Strathspey. Other valuable tracts of wild pinewoods occur in Glen Affric and parts of Deeside and Perthshire. It is a diverse habitat characterised by widely spaced Scots pines and a rich understorey of heather, blaeberry and juniper. Other typical plants include cowberry, chickweed wintergreen, lesser twayblade, twinflower and creeping lady's tresses orchid. In wetter margins, bog myrtle, grass-of-Parnassus and bog asphodel prosper. This is an intricate and delicately balanced environment, with many plants and trees depending upon complex and mutually beneficial relationships with fungi to extract vital nutrients from the soil.

As well as the crested tit, notable birds of these wild forests include the rare capercaillie and the endemic Scottish crossbill. Although the Scots pine is often regarded as the principal tree of our wildwoods, this is a mistaken perception, for wildwood simply means areas of woodland largely untouched by the hand of humanity and can comprise of any native species.

Birch is a keystone tree of such places, and the previous day I had visited a birch wood overlooking the nearby Insh Marshes, a sweeping oasis of bog, pools and watery channels stretching across Strathspey from the ruins of the eighteenth-century Ruthven Barracks in the south to near Aviemore in the north. The birches here have their own magical aura, with the woodland floor covered in a soft and spongy carpet of damp moss, coloured with every hue of green imaginable. I squeezed a clump of moss with my hand, and crystal-clear water dripped through my fingers, an elixir of life that ensures these woodlands are forever damp, even during prolonged dry spells. On the trunk of a birch above me, the brackets of several birch polypore fungi gained hold. Birch polypores parasitise birches, slowly drawing their life away and then thriving for many years after the tree has died, until the trunk has rotted completely away to windblown dust. Like most things in nature, there is reason and purpose for this, because the decaying birch provides life for numerous invertebrates and other types of fungi, and once the tree has fallen, sunlight filters to the woodland floor enabling plants – including birch seedlings – to prosper.

The birch is the ultimate pioneer, a trail-blazing species, often the first to colonise areas of cleared ground. The wind-blown seeds are easily spread and gain a tenacious grip in the soil to eventually form large tracts of scrubby woodland. As such, birch plays an important role in improving nutrient deficient land, its shed leaves helping to enrich the soil in preparation of the arrival of other trees fussier in their requirements. In some ways the birch is engaged in the tree equivalent of suicide because the eventual arrival of taller growing species such as oak and beech will ultimately shade them out.

As I wandered further through the Scots pines at Abernethy, my mind reflected upon the fact that there are remnants of wildwood all around us, for example, in steep ravines that have escaped the attention of grazing animals and are too inaccessible for tree felling that often consist of a wide mix of tree species including ash, aspen and rowan. Think too of the magnificent damp Atlantic oak woods of the Scottish west coast that are rich in ferns, mosses and liverworts. These ancient remnants are part of the great boreal forest – the world's largest forest ecosystem – that stretches across Scandinavia, Siberia and the northern part of North America.

At Abernethy, however, the Scots pine is king. There is something special about the Scots pine that is hard to define and as I ran my hand down the trunk of an old tree, my fingertips trembled under its rough texture, a haven of nooks and crannies for tiny invertebrates to hide. That the Scots pine is an imposing and attractive tree is inarguable, but it has something more. This is encapsulated in a lone Scots pine that I know in a remote Highland glen, which clings to a steep slope and is stunted in growth because of its exposed location. The presence of a sprawling golden eagle eyrie on one of the lower branches underlines the much bigger role the tree plays in our environment, a place where new life is created from within its hold.

Mature Scots pine woods are mesmerising places, with the trees having distinctive large flat-topped canopies and bark that can be markedly red or orange in places, especially towards the tops. Equally compelling are the lines of pines often found along the ridges of rounded hills that are used as shelter belts for sheep, and which form distinctive landmarks that can be seen from many miles away.

The Scots pine is indelibly ingrained in both our cultural and natural histories. It is Scotland's only large native conifer, however, the natural forest cover it once provided has undergone a quite startling reduction over the millennia because of the much-prized qualities of its wood, along with land being cleared for agriculture. The Scots pine has been a useful tree to humanity, providing top-quality timber that is easily worked and used for a wide range of products such as pit props, telegraph poles, building construction and furniture. As well as charcoal, the tree was a major source of turpentine, resin and tar. The cones, sometimes known as 'dead apples', made good kindling. Perversely, it was all these positive properties that contributed to its demise – rather than looking after our Scots pines as a renewable resource, they were mercilessly felled, leaving behind only fragments of their previous coverage.

This collapse is well summarised by Richard Mabey in *Flora Britannica* (1996) who wrote:

> *In medieval times, the great forest of native pine and birch stretched across most of the Highlands, from Perth to Ullapool. But from the late seventeenth century, it began to be ransacked, first to provide charcoal for lowland iron foundries, then to support the insatiable timber demands of the Napoleonic Wars. Any chance that the trees might regenerate was dashed by the notorious Highland Clearances in the eighteenth and nineteenth centuries and the blanketing of the denuded hills with sheep and later with deer. By the 1970s it was estimated that little more than 25,000 acres remained, much of it in small, scattered clumps.*

I continued my way through Abernethy Forest, not following a map but taking random turns along small tracks and paths, my mind becoming lost within its sublime vastness. Not too far from one path edge, a large mound of orangey-brown pine needles on the forest floor caught my eye. It was a wood ant nest and one of nature's true miracles. How can such tiny insects build such a magnificent structure?

It is my cardinal rule to never intentionally disturb wildlife, but nonetheless,
I could not resist gently placing my finger
on top of the nest to see how these
fascinating insects reacted to a potential
threat – an experiment, if you like. As
I suspected, their response was swift,
with several quickly swarming over my
finger and trying to bite it – although
their jaws were too small to inflict pain,
more a minor irritant. These workers
were mighty feisty, and if I were to

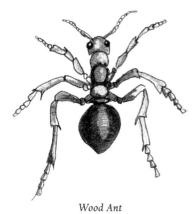

Wood Ant

miniaturise myself to their level, it would be like facing a pride of lions.

I withdrew my finger and sat cross-legged on a thick carpet of blaeberry
by this large domed nest, examining the busy activity of the wood ants
as they swarmed over the surface, constantly on the move. The dome was a
marvel of engineering, covered in a thatch of pine needles, small twigs and
other forest detritus, which keeps the nest dry and helps absorb solar energy,
ensuring the temperature of the nest is higher than the surroundings.

Somewhere deep inside will be the queen – or possibly several queens,
whose sole job is to lay eggs. Males are produced in spring, which will mate
with the queens, but the overall majority of ants are workers, which are
females that do not reproduce. Each worker has a specific job, some keep
the nest repaired, others forage for food, while many will tend the queen
and her brood.

It is a complex social set-up, a society where every ant has a place and
purpose. Indeed, the nest community could be likened to a single organism
but one made up of many different parts. The main food of wood ants is
sugary honeydew produced by aphids, which they have gleaned from the
sweet sap of Scots pines. In an intricate ecological adaptation, the worker
ants 'milk' the honeydew from the aphids. The developing ant brood also
require protein, and thus, a variety of insects are devoured, including those
that are tree pests. Wood ants are regarded by ecologists as one of the
pivotal species of these forests, given that they benefit the health of
woodlands in so many ways. For example, wood ants aid the dispersal of
native wild plant seeds by carrying them to new areas, with some of these

seed types containing a special substance to attract the ants. It is an intricate woodland web of life, with each element interacting upon the other. Take one part away and the rest crumbles.

The deadwood habitat provided by old or dead trees supports other rare insects, including the specialist hoverfly, *Callicera rufa*, which lays its eggs in holes formed in the rotting wood of old pine trees.

The weather was warm and flies buzzed around my head. I was reluctant to leave, for it had taken me a while to find this wood ant nest. I stayed a bit longer, absorbing the peace and tranquillity of the forest. A rather metallic repetitive call faintly broke the air which reminded me of clinking wine glasses. The noise gradually grew louder and over the pines bounded a small party of crossbills that soon disappeared into the distance. Crossbills are restless by nature and seldom stay still for long. They are handsome birds, especially the males with their vibrant brick-red plumage and deep bills that has led to them sometimes being likened to parrots. They are also one of our most specialist feeders, with their unique crossed-over bills intricately designed to extract the seeds from pinecones.

It is only in recent times that it has come to light that Scotland hosts three species of crossbill, including the Scottish crossbill, which is found nowhere else in the world (the other two are the common crossbill and the parrot crossbill). I do not have the expertise to tell them apart with certainty as they all look so similar, and all three species occur in Abernethy Forest.

The differences between them are subtle – the common crossbill generally has a slightly smaller bill in comparison to the others, the parrot crossbill the largest bill, and the Scottish crossbill is somewhere in-between. They also have slightly different calls and exhibit behavioural differences too, which reinforces mate selection and keeps hybridisation between the various types to a low level.

The common crossbill often travels across large distances and generally appears in Scotland in intermittent influxes from Europe in search of new feeding areas when the cone crop on the continent has failed. Good numbers will then stay here to breed but it is thought that many eventually drift back to Europe. The parrot crossbill is a specialist of Scots pine and also exhibits nomadic tendencies, although not nearly to the same degree as the common crossbill, whereas the Scottish crossbill is more sedentary and only undertakes small-scale movements within Scotland.

Scottish Crossbill

In a fascinating quirk of nature, each of the three types of crossbill have evolved slightly different breeding and feeding strategies. The parrot crossbill lays its eggs in February and March to time the fledging of the young when the cones of Scots pines start to open, thus making it easier for the youngsters to feed upon them. The Scottish crossbill tends to start breeding in March and the common crossbill in April in Scots pine woods, although the latter can breed at other times of the year because of its ability to exploit a variety of other conifers that produce seed at different times.

Such variations and their selection of mates of the same type are enough to classify them as different species. Such marginal differences in what is essentially the same type of bird may seem unimportant, but the exact opposite is the case, because change and evolution is going on around us all the time, which signifies nature's ability to adjust and adapt. Take the Scottish crossbill variant as an example. Like the parrot crossbill, it seems to prefer Scots pine, but in recent decades has begun to take advantage of maturing plantations of non-native species such as lodgepole pine. Here the cones are smaller and the seed easier to extract than those of Scots pine and there is the intriguing possibility that Scottish crossbills may even start to evolve slightly smaller bills as a result.

I had taken my caravan up to nearby Carrbridge, which provided the perfect base to explore the magnificent wildwoods of Strathspey — an opportunity to become truly acquainted with the ways of the forest. One exploration took me to a pair of remote woodland lochans that lay adjacent to one another. Perhaps lochan is too expansive a terminology, for they were large pools characterised by shallow water and brimming with aquatic vegetation. By the far side of the smaller one, I spotted several black and white ducklings scooting about on the surface. I knew instantly they were not mallard ducklings, as they are yellower and browner in colouration, and on bringing them into focus with my binoculars, I was thrilled to discover they were goldeneye ducklings, one of Scotland's scarcest breeding ducks.

A wave of worry coursed through my body. Where was the mother? These wee bundles of fluff were terribly exposed to attack from marauding gulls, crows and ravens. I watched the ducklings for about 20 minutes, becoming increasingly concerned about their fate. Perhaps the mother was on the other nearby and larger pool, which was about five minutes' walk away. I wandered over and sure enough, there she was gliding nonchalantly out on the water, where several herring gulls also milled about. I can only presume that the larger pool offered better feeding, and the mother had ventured there to refuel. It was an extremely risky thing to do, and her ducklings were in extreme peril without her guidance and protection. Unlike ducks such as mallards, goldeneyes can dive under the water, so the ducklings had that option for escape should a crow swoop down upon them. Given they were new to this world, I doubted whether they would have yet developed the reasoning to recognise danger, especially since they were confident with my presence and allowing me to approach close.

Goldeneyes are common winter visitors from breeding grounds in northern Europe but were only first recorded breeding in Scotland in 1970 at Loch an Eilein, near Aviemore. They lay their eggs in tree holes, and specially designed nest boxes have been erected in recent decades to encourage them to become established breeders. Despite this, the breeding population is small, perhaps only a hundred pairs nesting each year, concentrated mainly in Strathspey, but also in Deeside and a few other parts of the country.

The lochs and lochans of the wildwoods of Strathspey are sparkling, silvery oases and one of the special draws of the area. They are places where ospreys soar high in the skies above and dragonflies and damselflies flit by the boggy margins. Large red damselflies were especially abundant during my Strathspey woodland wanderings, even away from water, where like little flashes of delightful crimson, they brought colour to the woodland floor.

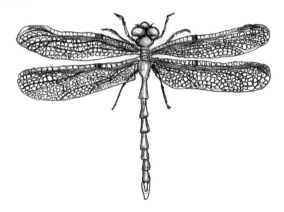

Large Red Damselfly

One morning in Rothiemurchus Forest, I embarked upon the popular tourist path along the edge of Loch an Eilein, before veering off to take a circuit of the smaller and more tranquil Loch Gamhna. Here, dazzling common blue and large red damselflies skimmed the water edges on weak and fluttering wings. Their erratic movements contrasted with the more purposeful and direct flight of four-spotted chaser dragonflies, which were also abundant. The flight of the four-spotted chasers was very precise and angular: forward, hover, sharp left, straight up, hard right and then back down again – the large eyes scanning the air for small flies to hunt down.

The two-paired wing arrangement of the four-spotted chaser ensures amazing agility, and they can manoeuvre like an attack helicopter by flying sideways and even backwards, as well as being capable of sudden forward surges of speed. It is this superlative aerial ability that makes dragonflies such deadly winged predators. Damselflies too are hunters of small insects.

At Loch Gamhna, the blue and red damselflies were intent on feverish mating, chasing one another and often coupling in the air. Once mated, the female damselfly lays her eggs in the water or on water vegetation, which hatch into six-legged carnivorous larvae (nymphs) that lurk on the bed of a pond or loch. They are voracious predators that seek out a wide range of invertebrate and other prey such as tadpoles and small fish. After a couple of years or more, the nymph crawls out of the water onto the stem of a plant and from its larval skin emerges a glistening adult winged insect. It is like the unfurling of a sparkling jewel. The contrast in lifestyle and difference in appearance between the larval and winged stage could hardly be greater, which is part of their appeal.

Dragonflies and damselflies have been described as birdwatchers' insects because their size and colour make them stand out from the crowd and they are easy to watch through binoculars. With their long pencil-thin bodies and multi-coloured hues, these wonderful creatures rival butterflies for their beauty.

Scotland holds three species of dragonfly that are found nowhere else in Britain: the northern damselfly, azure hawker and the northern emerald – underlining the important responsibility this country has for their conservation. At least two new breeding species – the emperor dragonfly and the banded demoiselle – have been added to the Scottish list in recent years, their colonisation from the south possibly due to climate change. This a double-edged sword with other more northern species that are on the edge of their range being threatened by such changes in our environment.

The fortunes of Scotland's dragonflies and damselflies depend upon the availability of suitable habitat, and this is where conservation efforts should be directed. These insects generally prefer still and running shallow freshwater areas, as well as open woodland, and the conservation of such areas not only benefits dragonflies but also a whole host of other fauna and flora.

On watching the iridescent flashes of the damsel and dragonflies whizzing across the water, I reflected that it was the insects that made these Strathspey wildwoods so special. The crested tits, capercaillies and crossbills get all the plaudits, but the insects were the driving force of much of the life here, and their colour and variety was a joy to behold. On paths and tracks by Boat of Garten, for example, I had found numerous green tiger beetles, their metallic, green-sheened carapaces glinting in the morning sunlight. They are fast and agile hunters, running across the ground to snap up spiders, caterpillars and ants in their fearsome jaws.

In these wildwoods, it is easy to visualise in the mind a goshawk swooping down upon a duck by a woodland lochan or a pine marten giving chase to a red squirrel, but the real action is happening at a more miniature level and largely unseen. Whether it be the miracle of wood ants 'milking' aphids for honeydew, the spectacular hunting dashes of dragonflies and damselflies or the death rush of a prowling green tiger beetle, the true drama of the wildwood lies in its spectacular invertebrates.

Chapter 17

A TREASURE TROVE OF LIFE BY THE MORAY FIRTH

June 2021 – The Black Isle

As I explored the shore of a remote section of the coast of the Black Isle, I stumbled upon a most unusual rock formation: old red sandstone exposed on the middle shore and segmented by narrow fissures to create a roughly divided but regular patchwork pattern of smooth cube-like shapes, which gently sloped down in a shelf towards the lapping low-tide waters of the Moray Firth.

This sloping shelf exhibited an unusual symmetry not often found on natural rock features, so I paused to examine the intricate geology of this remarkable stretch of coastline at Eathie, which lies between Rosemarkie and Cromarty. As I did so, it was easy to see why this was a place that inspired Hugh Miller, one of the most celebrated geologists of the nineteenth century, and where he spent much of his youth searching for fossils.

Eathie is one of the few onshore areas of Scotland where Jurassic rocks are exposed; within their bounds lies a rich prehistoric treasure of past life. Fossilised ammonites and shellfish are found here, but it is the fossil plants that have sparked most interest among researchers because of their excellent state of preservation, which has enabled their detailed study.

For me, fossils are as valuable as any antique from human history, and perhaps even more so, for they provide a record of past life that no longer exists, and a unique glimpse of the evolutionary processes that shaped the world of today. As I strolled along the shore, my inexpert eye was unable to catch sight of any fossils, but no matter, for this wild stretch of Moray coast was completely addictive, and despite the bright sunshine and the calm sea, there was not a soul to be seen.

My approach to the Eathie coast began at a small car park adjacent to the minor Black Isle coast road from Rosemarkie to Cromarty. From there, I followed a well-maintained path that dropped steeply down through woodland to the shore. The first part of the track passed an impressive beech trees, which stirred me to halt and admire their stature. White, the English eighteenth-century nature diarist, described ___ as, 'the most lovely of all forest trees, whether we consider its smooth rind or bark, its glossy foliage, or graceful pendulous boughs'.

How right he was, for a fully mature beech is both elegant and imposing. Beeches can live for several hundred years, and examining an old beech tree is like delving into a personal history, with the broken branches and deep splits and hollows highlighting the numerous storms survived over several human lifetimes. As autumn leaves turn and flutter to the ground, beech nuts will scatter upon the forest floor to be gorged upon by jays, squirrels and wood mice. The beech is a true giver of life.

On my descent to the shore, wood speckled butterflies fluttered in sun-dappled clearings and the frilly white petals of greater stitchwort sparkled and danced. The names of plants are intriguing, and often descriptive, with stitchwort being so-called because in the past it was used as a remedy for treating 'stitches' and similar pains in the abdomen.

This route down to the coast was well trodden by salmon nets-men until the early 1980s and on the shore there are the remains of an old fishing station. The salmon fishers used yairs or large nets strung out into the sea and staked in a crescent shape, which trapped the fish at low tide.

As I was exploring the old salmon station, the familiar hump-back of a bottlenose dolphin rolled across the surface of the sea about half a kilometre or so away. The Moray Firth was flat and serene, so I sat and watched the dolphin for several minutes as it slowly worked its way down the coast towards Rosemarkie. Earlier in the day, I had dropped in at Chanonry Point, near Rosemarkie, which is renowned as being one of the best places in Scotland for seeing bottlenoses, attracted by salmon, sea trout and mackerel funnelling into the narrow passage found in the firth here, which is flanked on the southern side by the imposing structure of Fort George. There is no such thing as predictable wildlife watching, and despite persistent scanning of the narrows, no dolphins appeared. This lone dolphin at Eathie, however, was ample compensation, and one which brought back vivid memories of the animals I had seen off the mouth of Aberdeen Harbour a few weeks previously.

There were other creatures out in the firth too, including a couple of cormorants. As I walked northwards along the shore, another cormorant

Cormorant (Eathie)

rested in lazy style on the rocks. On nearing it, the bird began to eye me nervously, unsure whether to take flight, or to stay put in the hope that I might move on. In the end the bird compromised, awkwardly sliding off its rocky perch and disappearing down into a bowl-shaped depression in the rocks where I could no longer see it. It was almost as if the cormorant had adopted an 'out of sight, out of mind' philosophy. A fleeting and mischievous temptation crossed my mind to creep close to where the cormorant lay hidden, and then peer over the rocks to surprise it, but I quickly suppressed such boyish instincts.

It is said that beauty lies in the eyes of the beholder, and at first glance even the most gracious would find it challenging to concede any attractive physical qualities in the cormorant, especially when seen silhouetted with wings outstretched like a crucifix against an evening sky where its dark, almost pterodactyl-like, form borders on the sinister. Certainly, the overwhelming blackness of cormorant plumage has resulted in the bird traditionally being associated with evil and greed. The name cormorant dates to the fourteenth century and owes its origin to the Latin for sea raven – another bird that has long been treated with suspicion. In his epic poem, 'Paradise Lost', John Milton portrayed Satan himself breaking into Paradise and sitting on the Tree of Life 'like a cormorant'; and Shakespeare's play *Richard II* refers to the gluttony associated with the bird.

A short distance further along the shore, a pair of great black-backed gulls rested upon a grass-topped rock stack. It was possible they had a nest here, but it looked more likely they were youngish non-breeders that were building up a pair bond, perhaps in readiness to breed next year. Like the cormorant, I imagine many people would regard great black-backed gulls as having the look of the brute about them. I find their strength and power compelling, and the stark contrast between their charcoal wings and back, against the snow-white head and underparts, strangely alluring. Great black-backed gulls are like raptors of the sea, a top predator and scavenger of our marine environment.

On the distant southern shore of the Moray Firth, a long shimmering sandy shore gleamed, stretching from Nairn to Findhorn. I had visited this magnificent sandy beach only the day before and had been buoyed by its broad expanses and wild emptiness. Here, there were offshore sandbars and spits and large expanses of sand-dune and saltmarsh. Beyond the tidal sandbars in slightly deeper waters lie submerged sandbanks, which are vital nursery areas for juvenile fish.

Oystercatcher (Eathie Bothy)

Further along the shoreline at Eathie I put to flight a pair of oystercatchers, 'kleeping' noisily as they swirled above me on slow-flapping wings. They had chicks hidden somewhere nearby and their displeasure at my intrusion was obvious. Oystercatchers are among Scotland's more striking birds, with their long orange-red bills and contrasting black and white plumage. They have adapted better than most other waders to the ever-increasing encroachment of human activity on our landscape, and have even embraced urbanisation by nesting on the flat-topped roofs of buildings in towns and feeding in parks and playing fields. Oystercatchers are one of those birds that it is hard not to adore, and when camping in the Highlands in spring and early summer, it is the noise of 'piping' oystercatchers that sends me to sleep and the same call that stirs me at dawn.

I mentioned in a previous chapter about the distraction display of a red grouse in the Cairngorms – trailing its wing as if injured to lure me away from his mate with her chicks. One of the most extreme forms of this behaviour I have ever witnessed was demonstrated by an oystercatcher. Several years ago, when driving slowly along a small country road in Deeside, an oystercatcher appeared on the tarmac right in front of the moving car and madly flapped and dragged one of its wings along the ground, keeping ahead of me all the while as I pressed the brake and slowed to a snail's pace. The oystercatcher must have had chicks hiding in the grassy verge, and to this brave mother the car was a dangerous predator, and by feigning injury she was hoping to draw it away. It was a case of David and Goliath and a vivid illustration of the extent a mother will go to protect her young.

It did not take long before I had moved far enough away from the pair of oystercatchers at Eathie for them to calm down and the air to become quiet once more. A rich, narrow strip of grass and wild-flowers sandwiched the top-shore and the steep scarp that rose high

Small Pearl-Bordered Fritillary

above the beach, and here small pearl-bordered fritillary butterflies flitted and spiralled on powerful, orange-patterned wings. They are exquisite little butterflies, full of the zest of life, and seldom staying still for any length of time.

The alarm call of a blackbird rang out and a female sparrowhawk flashed along the foot of the scarp on fast beating wings, swooping and weaving like a guided missile. She was on a mission – a smash and grab raid to flush out a songbird and snatch it from the air with her razor-sharp talons. She was gone in a flash, leaving panic in her wake, with frightened blackbirds and blue tits chattering with fraught anguish. The birds soon settled, and calm returned once more.

The sun was shining brightly, and the air was warm, so with no-one else about on this lonely shore, I stripped off and gingerly lowered myself onto a submerged rock shelf by the water's edge, where I sat half under the water with the sea lapping my chest. Around me were several crimson jelly-blobbed beadlet anemones, which had clustered in a rock crevice. I gently brushed my finger against the rough and sticky tentacles of one, which were quickly retracted. The tentacles are used to catch small creatures such as shrimps and contain nematocysts which act like tiny harpoons, triggered by touch and injecting their prey with venom. Fortunately, they are not strong enough to be detected by the touch of a human finger and I was in no danger of being stung.

It was wonderfully relaxing sitting on my half-submerged perch, but after a while the cold got the better of me, and I reluctantly emerged from the water, shivering yet invigorated. I had not visited this stretch of the Moray Firth coast before. The diversity of its natural treasures between the land and the sea left me elated and vowing to return.

Chapter 18

WHALES, PORPOISES AND
FLYING SEA TROLLS

June 2021 – The Minch

Whilst I had dipped into Scotland's underwater marine world when snorkelling and had carefully trodden along shorelines in search of wading birds and other fauna and flora during this wildlife journey, I was aware that there were numerous natural riches further out to sea, which had remained tantalisingly out of reach. Indeed, as my Scottish wildlife adventure progressed, it was becoming increasingly apparent that it was the influence of the sea that defined Scotland's nature, the driving force that ensures this small country on the wild Atlantic edge is such a special place. Accordingly, when embarking on the next stage of my travels to the Outer Hebrides, it was the ferry trip across the Minch which excited me as much as the anticipation of exploring the mountains of Harris and the flower-spangled machair of South Uist.

I adore travelling on ferries, and on embarking the CalMac ferry MV *Hebrides* for the almost two-hour voyage from Uig in Skye to Tarbert in Harris, I hurried to an outside viewing deck – for I suspected I was in store for a spectacular wildlife treat. I was especially enlivened because the sea was unusually calm, a flat reflective mirror, which dramatically increased the likelihood of detecting whales, porpoises and dolphins. The Minch abounds with these marvellous animals, but when the sea is wave-crested, their rolling backs and fins are hard to discern.

The sea sparkled silver under the diffuse rays of sunshine that filtered through a high veil of languid cloud. There was hardly a whisper of wind, and as the ferry pulled away from Uig under the surge of its powerful, rumbling engines, such was the tranquillity of the water, I could discern the gentle rippling on the water surface created by a shoal of sprats as they swirled and tumbled just beneath. A shag roll-dived further out and herring gulls wheeled and soared above the ferry on lazy wings. On the Waternish peninsula, the long linear row of white houses in the hamlet of Gillen reflected the soft morning light.

My anticipation soon bore fruit, and before the ferry had passed Waternish Point, several porpoises had materialised, their shallow arch-backed rolls only marginally breaking the water's surface. Porpoises are the most common whale and dolphin species (collectively known as cetaceans) found off our shores, as well as being the smallest, being less than 2m long. They are shy creatures and will avoid vessels, unlike dolphins which often approach close to boats out of curiosity and fun, and even ride their bow waves.

Although porpoises are common, it is thought their numbers are in decline, a sad testimony to the many threats facing our marine environment, including pollution and climate change. Porpoises are not as sociable as many other cetaceans, tending to hang around in small loose groups, individually, or in mother and calf pairs, hunting for shoaling fish such as sandeels, sprats and herring. Unlike whales, the blow of a porpoise is seldom seen, but it can sometimes be heard and sounds like a sneeze, which has earned the creature the alternative name of puffing pig.

I recall once finding a dead porpoise on Balmedie beach, north of Aberdeen, and being awe-struck by the sleek beauty of the creature. The skin was like polished ebony, the rounded face benign and attractive. It was a silken torpedo, perfectly designed for its oceanic life in search of fish. Despite its cold, lifeless form, this was a warm-blooded animal that exuded intelligence and character, and a wave of sadness swept across me as I gently brushed my fingertips across its smooth skin.

As the ferry left Loch Snizort and the Skye shore behind and began its traverse of the Minch, a much larger rolling back broke the water off the port bow – a minke whale. As quick as it had surfaced, the animal dived. 'Please reappear', I intoned silently. Thankfully, it did so once more, this time astern of the vessel, where its sickle-shaped fin, set well back on the body, appeared several more times until the animal faded into the distance. Against the far backdrop of Dunvegan Head on Skye, another minke whale broke the surface, the sea surging all around in dark waves and ripples. Minkes are the most frequently encountered whale off the Scottish west coast, and on calm days can even be spotted from the shore – rocky headlands offering the best vantage points.

Minkes are sleeker and smaller in length than most other whales. Because of their small size for a whale (an adult is about 8m long),

Minke Whale

minke whales were not targeted by Scottish and Irish whalers until the start of the twentieth century when the numbers of other larger species had begun to diminish. Cetaceans are now fully protected around our shores, but perversely Norway and Japan continue to hunt whales – in some instances, in the recent past, ostensibly under the cover of a 'scientific quota' for research, but in reality, driven by a reluctance to relinquish the dwindling market for whale meat and products. For 2021, Norway set an annual kill quota of 1,278 minke whales, which was a self-allocated quota and unchanged from 2020. Iceland still has a self-imposed whale 'quota'. Fortunately, whaling seems to have ebbed away there in recent years and may now have come to an end.

The killing of such magnificent and intelligent creatures is inexplicable and unforgivable, especially since the method of capture with explosive-grenade harpoons causes incredible pain and anguish. One can only imagine the horror of the underwater death-throe cries of a harpooned whale, and the distress it must cause to other whales in the vicinity. The continuation of whaling is a dark stain upon the soul of humanity.

The minke whale name is derived from an eighteenth-century Norwegian whaler, *Meincke*, although it does have the alternative, although not often used, name of 'lesser roqual'. In reference to this, renowned Scotland-based naturalist and rewilder, Roy Dennis, pointed out in his book, *Cottongrass Summer* (2020):

> *When I see one of these wonderful animals in the seas*
> *around the Scottish coasts, I prefer to use 'lesser roqual' than*
> *commemorate the name of a long-gone Norwegian whaler.*

Around Scottish shores, minke whales face their own set of threats, including becoming entangled in fishing gear and being killed in collisions with ships. Minke whales lunge feed for fish, where they move at speed through the water, before turning on their side and scooping up prey such as herring and sprats into their wide-open mouths. As such, they are apex predators at the top of the food chain and are vulnerable to the accumulation of ocean pollutants in their bodies, such as polychlorinated biphenyls (PCBs). These toxic chemical compounds were once manufactured in vast quantities, and although banned decades ago, they are persistent in our environment, and can impact upon the reproduction success of whales and supress their immune systems. The orcas (killer whales) that live on the west coast of Scotland, for example, are now down to a handful of individuals and they have not produced a calf in a quarter of a century, a tragic ticking timebomb of regional extinction on our doorstep.

As well as minke whales and the porpoises, there were other forms of oceanic life visible from the ferry that gripped my attention, most notably Manx shearwaters, which wheeled low over the sea on narrow, outstretched wings. It was almost as if they were powered by some invisible force, for they barely flapped their wings, yet skidded low over the sea surface at tremendous speed, the aerodynamics of their wings utilising the smallest of updrafts and breeze eddies. Manx shearwaters are true oceanic nomads, visiting our shores in spring and summer to breed, and spending the winter in the South Atlantic, principally off South America, feeding on small squid, fish and free-swimming crustaceans. They are renowned for their navigational skills and after flying thousands of kilometres on their spring migration, will often unerringly return to the same nesting burrow as used the year before.

Manx shearwaters nest on a handful of islands off the west and north of Scotland, with the breeding colony on Rum being the largest in the world, and Scotland as a whole holding a third of the world population. On Rum,

Manx Shearwater (Waternish)

shearwaters breed on four mountain tops at altitudes of between 450m and 700m. The names of these mountains are Norse in origin, and one of them, Trollval, is possibly so called because the Vikings believed there to be trolls living under the soil – which were in fact shearwaters in their burrows making their strange, haunting calls.

Breeding shearwaters may travel large distances from their nesting colony in search of food, and when they return, they do so at night, with large rafts of birds assembling offshore, before flying to their nesting burrows after sunset. Shearwaters are mystical, and as I watched these trolls of the sea swirling and weaving low over the Minch, it was hard to grasp in the mind the huge distances that they roam over their lifetimes.

As the coast of Harris neared, a small dark flickering close to the sea surface caught my eye. It was a storm petrel, a diminutive seabird not much larger than a sparrow, with sooty plumage and a white rump, which gave it an appearance somewhat akin to a house martin. Like the Manx shearwater, the storm petrel is an oceanic wanderer, gleaning small crustaceans, fish larvae and other tiny planktonic creatures from the sea surface, or by shallow diving. It is the world's smallest seabird, a paperweight bundle of fragility but with an inner toughness that can endure the harshest of storms. After breeding on Scottish islands, storm petrels spend the winter in waters off southern Africa.

Storm Petrel

The storm petrel flying close to the ferry hovered in search of food in a buoyant and bobbing flight, pit-pattering its feet across the sea surface. It was almost as if it was walking upon water, and sailors in the past called the bird 'Little Peter' in reference to St Peter, from the Christian Bible, who strived to walk across the waves.

The short ferry trip to Harris had revealed a plethora of life, and my return journey, which was on the more northerly route between Stornoway, in Lewis, to Ullapool on the mainland, also reaped rewards. The sea was rougher and for much of the way I was unable to spot any cetaceans due to the conditions. As the vessel approached the Summer Isles at the mouth of Loch Broom on the approach to Ullapool, the water quickly calmed.

The signs were looking good – and so it proved, for a short while later, the ferry swept past a large pod of common dolphins, their pale flanks catching the sunshine each time they breached the water, sending my mind spinning with enthralled excitement. Common dolphins are slenderer in build compared with the much chunkier bottlenose dolphins, and are very sociable, congregating in large pods where they leap and porpoise in spectacular splashes, often working together to herd fish.

The dolphins were heading out of the loch, and with the ferry steaming fast the other way towards Ullapool, their splashes and swirls in the water soon disappeared into the vastness of the horizon. Whales and dolphins are an oft-forgotten part of Scottish nature because they are so seldom encountered. By the simple step of entering their world and utilising Scotland's ferry network, there is every chance of spotting them and gaining unique glimpses into their secret lives.

Chapter 19

THE GLORY OF THE FLOWER-RICH MACHAIR

June 2021 – South Uist

Polka-dotted with the golden blooms of buttercups and silverweed, this wondrous machair on South Uist near Loch Druidibeg stretched as far as the eye could see, a gleaming carpet of life that brimmed with the wild calls of breeding waders. This was heaven on earth, the air crystal clear, the sun shining warmly, and only the gentlest of breezes ruffling the grasses and abundant wildflowers. A lapwing took to the air on broad, floppy wings and wheeled above me, calling 'pee-wee, pee-wee' all the while. It had chicks nearby and was concerned by my presence, trying to draw me away with its persistent low passes.

Another bird called, a rattling purr, unfamiliar in tone and one which I did not immediately recognise. A small brown wader materialised in the short tangle of grass and wildflowers ahead of me – a dunlin, looking resplendent with its lightly streaked fawn breast and black underbelly.

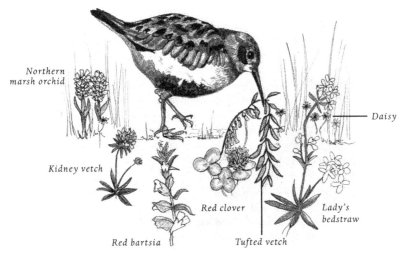

Dunlin & Plants

Dunlins are charismatic little birds, often seen by our shorelines in winter in large wheeling flocks but are much less frequently encountered on their summer breeding grounds on the remote hills and coasts of northern and western Scotland.

A redshank was also making its presence felt, perched on a fence post, uttering short, high-pitched calls. A pair of oystercatchers lingered not too far away, their black and white plumage contrasting starkly with the green, flower-patterned machair.

Corncrake (The Uists)

Then, the strangest of noises – a rasping, frog-like 'crek, crek' – from deep within a damp flush where a sweep of yellow flag irises prospered. A corncrake had spoken and fallen swiftly silent once more. A summer visitor from Africa, the corncrake is a mysterious and secretive bird. Not much bigger than a mistle thrush, they are scarce breeders in Scotland, confined mainly to the Hebrides and Orkney. Related to coots and moorhens, but adopting a dry-land existence, they lurk in thick grass and other vegetation, with their brown cryptic plumage making them extremely difficult to spot. Old field systems and farming methods suit their needs perfectly, enabling them to forage for small invertebrates and seeds, and into the late nineteenth and early twentieth centuries corncrakes thrived in many parts of Scotland. In the early 1800s, corncrakes were often heard in the centre of Edinburgh, nesting in areas of long grass, such was their ubiquity.

Rapid decline in corncrake numbers has ensued over the last hundred years or so, linked to the introduction of mechanised hay mowing and the losses of nests and chicks that inevitably followed. To counter this, corncrake-friendly farming measures have been encouraged in their last outposts since the 1990s, including government schemes to encourage crofters to delay mowing of hay and silage fields and the provision and safeguarding of tall vegetation for this notoriously shy bird to shelter in spring and summer. As a result, numbers gradually increased, but in recent years the population has begun to slowly dwindle once more, possibly because of reasons connected with their wintering grounds. Corncrakes, it would seem, are complex birds with particular needs.

I listened out for a bit longer, in the hope that the corncrake would call again. It never did. It was late morning; corncrakes generally rasp their strange calls between dusk and dawn. Hearing this bird was an unexpected bonus, its presence a vivid reminder of the importance of the machair to creatures and plants.

I sat on a lichen-encrusted boulder and absorbed the wildness of the environment. Behind me, and to the east, lay the triangular top of Hecla, the island's second highest mountain. As I turned my head, the distinctive divided geography of South Uist shone out at me, with the east typified by hilly, heather uplands and the west comprising low-lying fertile coastal machair and vast sweeps of sandy beaches. Machair is a Gaelic word and means a fertile low-lying grassy plain. The underlying substrate of this machair is comprised of calcareous rich shell-sand, blown-in from the wild Atlantic over the millennia, creating one of the world's rarest habitats – one which characterises the western fringes of the Uists and other exposed western coasts of Scotland and Ireland. The shell-sand is the magic ingredient with its alkaline nature neutralising the acid from the peaty soil to create a fertile environment.

Such areas have been low-intensity grazed and tilled by crofters for generations, creating a rich landscape where wildflowers and bumblebees abound, including the scarce great yellow bumblebee. The machair provides a colour tapestry that never fails to impress. Its future, however, hangs in the balance through pressure to improve efficiency and modernise farming practices, which can only be stemmed through the provision of agri-environment funding support to encourage the status quo.

Rather than just comprising flower-rich grasslands, machair is in reality a mosaic of different habitats, comprising beach, sand dunes, pasture, bogs, ditches and lochs, each one inter-linking with the other, and which gradually rolls and merges into the peaty moorland and hills further east.

The machair is attractive to breeding waders for a variety of reasons. The vegetation is high enough to hide nests but still low cropped to a sufficient level to enable adults and chicks to forage. The proximity of the sandy shore is another bonus, providing valuable additional areas for waders to probe for invertebrates, especially when the young reach the flying stage. It is the absence of mammalian predators such as stoats, weasels and foxes, however, which is the underlying reason ground-nesting waders can prosper here. When hedgehogs were introduced to the Uists in the 1970s, they became a serious predator of wader eggs, and over the last couple of decades have been subject to a control programme to restore the natural balance. The scheme has often stoked controversy, especially in the earlier stages when animals were culled; more latterly animals have been removed and translocated to other areas on the mainland.

There are, of course, avian predators of wader eggs and chicks such as ravens, gulls and birds of prey, and earlier that day, I had watched, spellbound, as a short-eared owl quartered a section of heather moorland further north. Short-eared owls are unusual for owls in that they fly during daylight hours, methodically quartering and examining the ground in their quest for small prey.

As I was about to rise from my rocky resting place, a harsh 'kark, kark' filled the air. I glanced up just in time to glimpse a red-throated diver swoop overhead on fast-beating wings. It was heading towards its fishing grounds out at sea, the urgency of the flight indicating that it had hungry youngsters to feed, which were probably lying low by the edge of a nearby lily-fringed hill lochan.

A pair of twittering twites – small linnet-like finches – bounded through the air in an undulating flight, before alighting on a wire fence. They are attractive birds with a bewitching beauty and yet my eyes were drawn to the ground, for there were daisies everywhere, stretching in a flowing, white-speckled sea across the machair. If I were to nominate our most inspiring wildflower, the daisy would be right there at the top, for it is a beautiful little plant with the toughest of hearts. Here, on the machair, they are continually grazed, while on garden lawns in deepest suburbia they are brutally trimmed by lawnmowers week in, week out. Yet only a few days after being cropped, they are back out again in their white-flowering magnificence.

Such punishment is no problem for daisies, for they love short-cropped grass as it provides the perfect conditions for them to thrive. Let the grass grow long and the daisies will be gone. The daisy is also remarkable in that there is barely a month in the year when there are not at least some daisies out in flower, even in darkest winter. The name daisy is a derivation of day's eye, which reflects the yellow orb revealed when the delicate white petals open in the morning, and which resembles the sun. And, of course, daisies are a magnet for insects, attracting a range of pollinators.

There was a rich proliferation of other wildflowers on the ground that stretched before me. Typical species that thrive on the machair include red and white clover, tufted vetch, kidney vetch, red bartsia, eyebright, lady's bedstraw and different types of orchids. The delicate pink-red flowers of red bartsia are especially attractive, and eyebright is another little gem that forever draws me in. When one is standing up, eyebright is hardly noticeable – registering as no more than diminutive pale flecks in the grass, but get down close, and the flowers are pearls of brilliance, featuring yellow blotches in their centres, from which subtle purple lines radiate out.

Another facet that struck me about the South Uist machair was the abundance of starlings. Many birds had just fledged from their nests and large creches of youngsters foraged on these rich meadow lands, often bickering among each other, their sharp beaks jabbing excitedly into the grass as they sought out grubs living just beneath the surface. This was the perfect place for starlings to thrive: insect-rich grasslands combined with nearby crofts where they can nest in roof crevices. On adjacent beaches, rotting kelp along the strandline abound with sand flies and other invertebrates for starlings to feast upon. Starlings and their busy lifestyles are appealing to watch, and they are such comical birds, too. Starlings are great mimics and once when on holiday in Spain, I awoke every morning to one that copied with uncanny accuracy the chirruping noise made by nocturnal cicadas. Over the years, I have come across Scottish starlings that have mimicked screeching owls and the yodelling of green woodpeckers.

As I returned from the coastal machair towards the eastern side of Loch Druidibeg – a sprawling, convoluted freshwater loch that straddles the centre-part of South Uist – my senses were continually drawn by white waterlilies, which scattered the surface of many surrounding pools and lochans. They were on the verge of emerging into their full floral splendour, and the large snowy-white petals, centred by a golden ball of brilliance, provided dazzling contrast to the dark, peaty water from which they emerged. White waterlilies are prolific in the lochans of the Outer Hebrides and their ecological importance is immense, providing shelter for trout and a vast array of invertebrates.

White Waterlilies

My base for the week was on Harris, and with the Berneray to Leverburgh ferry to catch, I hastened on my way from Loch Druidibeg, travelling across causeways to Benbecula, Grimsay and then North Uist, before following the westerly circuit road. Not far from the small settlement of Baile Mhàrtainn, and away out in the Atlantic, a grey shadow caught the corner of my eye. I pulled into a layby and drew out my binoculars. On the far horizon lay the magical islands of St Kilda, home to their own sub-species of wren and field mouse, the products of evolutionary isolation. Standing clear and proud, and where throngs of seabirds nest, my binoculars brought this remote archipelago tantalisingly close, almost as if I were being flirted with and teased. I pulled the binoculars regretfully away from my eyes: 'One day I will step upon your shores, I vowed, one day'.

Chapter 20

JELLYFISH SWARMS AND INSPIRING SEA EAGLES

June 2021 – Harris

There is something wonderfully hypnotic about gliding over a kelp forest, the large brown-green fronds swaying in gentle unison with the tidal current in such an enchanting manner that one is drawn deep within its seductive hold.

I had only been snorkelling for a short while in Loch Chliuthair in south east Harris, but already I had glimpsed several types of fish, including shoals of saithe, as well as corkwing and rock cook wrasse using their pectoral or side fins to scull through the kelp with ease and agility. This kelp bed was as rich in life as any tropical rainforest, and within its realm lay hordes of creatures, including anemones, sea urchins, sea squirts, sponges, lobsters and a vast array of different molluscs.

Kelp forests are exceptionally biodiverse because they provide shelter and places for creatures to settle and gain an anchor-hold. In many ways, Scottish kelp forests are an equivalent to coral reefs, providing similar essential ecosystem benefits to the inshore marine environment.

I flicked my flippers a few more times and drifted into a deep fissure that cut into a rockface by the sea edge. It was a dark and eerie place and a wave of apprehension swept over me; probably for no other reason than I had entered the unknown, which made me feel uncomfortable. I slowed my breathing and relaxed the mind – that was better, I must be getting soft I thought, for I had never felt angst before when snorkelling. I began to look around me, marvelling at the colourful sponges on the sides of the rock cleft. Below me, a pair of brown crabs scuttled across the seabed. Then, a movement near where the crabs had scurried – a stunning blue jellyfish, which began to move slowly to the surface, its umbrella-shaped bell pulsing like a slow beating heart.

The purple blue of its cap contrasted starkly with the white trailing stinging tentacles, which shone and luminesced like a glowing beam. The jellyfish hung near the surface for a short while before slowly descending again. I have noticed this behaviour before with blue jellyfish, rising up and down the water column, which is possibly a feeding strategy to glean plentiful plankton.

Blue Jellyfish

On manoeuvring out of the rock gully to continue my snorkel, several other blue jellyfish appeared, along with an impressive lion's mane jellyfish, with a massive red-hued umbrella top and long hanging stingers.

On the final approach to my exit point on a nearby sloping rock shelf, a swarm of moon jellyfish appeared before my facemask, so distinctive with their shallow saucer-shaped bodies, with four rings in the centre of their bells. There had been strong winds the previous day, and this was a raft of dead and dying animals that had been consumed by the surge.

Moon jellyfish are fringed with tiny tentacles that are harmless, so I slowly glided in among the creatures, wallowing in what was effectively a thick jellyfish soup, a marine graveyard and a stark reminder of the deadly power of the sea. The appearance of large swarms of jellyfish is a regular occurrence off Scottish coasts in summer, and in this instance, I am certain the unusually cool spring, followed by a much warmer spell had created the perfect conditions for a sudden planktonic bloom, which in turn had resulted in an explosion in jellyfish numbers. Only the day before, I had stumbled upon a large barrel jellyfish, a species I have only occasionally encountered when snorkelling in west of Scotland waters before. It is entirely possible that climate change may make such regular swarming of jellyfish a more frequent occurrence.

The previous day when snorkelling, a most unusual creature appeared – a free-swimming isopod, which took an attraction to me and settled on my left-hand wetsuit glove. This marine isopod was a relative of the woodlouse, so commonly found under logs in gardens, but was about three-times larger and orange in colour. It crawled over my glove and between my fingers for a short while, before embarking upon its watery travels once more, swimming away in an awkward, almost comical fashion.

Harris is such a diverse and dramatic area of the Outer Hebrides, with its vast sandy beaches on the west side, the wild, almost moonscape, rocky environment in eastern parts, and the towering mountains of the north. The azure sea that laps the pristine sandy beaches of Luskentyre and Scarista in South Harris has inspired artists for generations, not just for the shape and form of the landscape, but equally so for the ever-changing light created by weather systems sweeping-in off the Atlantic. No two days are ever the same, and the panorama ebbs and flows as part of nature's poetic power.

When on Harris, I resided on the island's east side near the hamlet of Cluer, which stands at the head of Loch Chliuthair. From the northern flank of the loch, a marvellous scene unfolds down to South Uist, and to the east, the Skye shoreline is easily visible on clear days. On one unusually warm and sunny evening, as I gazed out to sea close to one of the headlands that guards the mouth of the loch, a commotion in the sky brought me out of a dreamy reverie. A huge bird was rapidly approaching from the south, mercilessly hounded by a much smaller bird. In an instant, I knew I was witnessing something remarkable. The larger bird was an impressive sea eagle, and its persistent attacker was a common gull, calling incessantly and mobbing the eagle in a bid to drive it away. Within the blink of an eye, the pair swooped so low over me that I could clearly discern the pale, piercing eyes of the eagle, the intricate arrangements of its wing feathers, along with its sun-glinted, wedge-shaped white tail. In a flash, they were gone, the angry gull calls rapidly fading across the warm sea air. Such was the sheer surprise and drama of the occasion that I hardly drew a breath for several seconds, my mind in a turmoil of excitement.

It might seem strange for the much smaller gull to put its life at risk by persistently pestering the eagle, but such behaviour is common among many birds when they see a raptor, and who rely on their agility to ensure there is little danger of the tables being turned. This gull may have had chicks nearby, and its swooping attacks were more than enough to distract the eagle's attention.

White-tailed Eagle, or Sea Eagle

The gull's behaviour was fascinating, but it was the majesty of the sea eagle that had enthralled me most, with its huge wingspan and powerful beak still imprinted clearly upon my mind. Also known as the white-tailed eagle, these dramatic birds were persecuted to extinction in Scotland by the beginning of the twentieth century. A pioneering reintroduction scheme began in 1975 with eaglets being released on Rum in the Inner Hebrides. The first successful breeding took place in 1985. Further releases in the 1990s in Wester Ross ensured that the population became self-sustaining. A follow-up reintroduction scheme on the east of Scotland has also taken place, with these birds now slowly becoming established.

Today, there are well over 100 breeding pairs in Scotland, and numbers are increasing each year.

Sea eagles are controversial, especially among sheep farmers, and there is no doubt that they do sometimes take lambs. When I waxed lyrical about the magnificence of sea eagles in Skye in one of my weekly 'Nature Watch' columns in *The Press & Journal*, the piece attracted several angry responses from readers because I had failed to mention lamb predation. These complaints were fair comment because, to provide balance, I should have mentioned that sea eagles do take lambs. Whether such losses are significant is a question to which I have no answer. One reader told me they have a significant impact on hill farmers in Skye, and another said that the people who had reintroduced sea eagles were themselves guilty of a wildlife crime, not least because these birds were also impacting upon the local population of golden eagles.

I do not know whether there is credence to either point. Sea eagles belong here and have done so since the dawn of time until they were wiped out. Biodiversity is the cornerstone of our survival, and with it declining year-on-year at a frightening rate, humanity has a responsibility to protect and nurture our wild creatures and plants, otherwise we will cause irreversible harm to our planet, and ultimately ourselves. Sometimes that can lead to conflict, nonetheless we need to find ways of managing and living with that, where nature, farming and other legitimate land use can coexist in harmony. We need food on our plates, but we also need a healthy and diverse ecosystem.

If there were ever a national opinion poll on sea eagles, I am certain the result would be universally in favour of their reintroduction, and this majority are the consumers to whom farmers are selling their produce — cognisance should be taken of that fundamental fact. Sea eagles deliver tangible tourism benefits, bringing income to businesses throughout the Highlands and Islands. An environmentally healthy and diverse environment is both desirable and an economic asset that creates jobs.

The following day, I ventured to the far south-west of Harris, taking a track from the small settlement of Taobh Tuath to the ruined medieval chapel at Rubh' an Teampaill. The first part of the walk passed through rich machair, reminding me of my visit to South Uist only a few days previously. Here, the air was filled with the welcoming calls of waders, and a fast-flying snipe weaved away into the air from a damp margin where it had been hiding.

Soon, the track reached the coast, overlooking the fine sandy beach at Tràigh na Cleabhaig, which was fringed by an aquamarine sea. Backdropped by sand-dunes, the panorama across the sound of Harris to Berneray was inspiring, with numerous islands, islets and rocky reefs lying in between, the largest of which was Pabbay. There must be an abundance of natural marine treasures thriving around these skerries, I thought, which would prove exciting places to explore. I also wondered whether waders and seabirds nested on some of these islets. If they did, given the abundance of small islands, their environmental importance would be immense.

A screeching noise filled the air above as an Arctic tern swooped low over me, before taking a wide turn back towards the beach and over the sand-dunes. Arctic terns are such graceful birds, with their slender bodies, long wings and fork tails. It is entirely appropriate for these dainty birds (as well as common terns) to be described as sea swallows. I scanned the upper beach with my binoculars and spotted another tern resting on the sand. Did it have a nest? Yes, it almost certainly did, and with other terns excitedly milling about over the sand-dunes, it looked like there was a small breeding colony. This area is popular with beach walkers and the nesting terns were extremely vulnerable to disturbance by both people and their dogs. Although Arctic terns are delicate in appearance, they are feisty birds and will relentlessly mob and dive-bomb any unwelcome intruder that should venture onto their nesting grounds. For the moment, the beach was empty, and the terns were at peace with the world.

It is an enjoyable experience to watch an Arctic tern when fishing, with its characteristic slow flight, head continually looking downwards, sometimes pausing in the air for a brief hover, before plummeting down into the sea and emerging with a silvery sprat or other small fish in its scarlet, dagger-like bill. Arctic terns are especially fascinating because of the huge distances they travel over their lifetime, and it seemed incredible that the birds on this Harris beach may only a few months previously have been foraging around the pack ice off the fringes of Antarctica. Arctic terns are, in effect, perpetual migrants that only stop for a few months to breed and which otherwise continually follow the lure of summer whether it be in the Northern or Southern Hemisphere.

I left the terns behind me, and skirted around two smaller, sandy beaches before reaching the crumbled chapel at Rubh' an Teampaill. There was a Viking construction on the site before the chapel was built, and earlier still, an Iron Age broch (defensive tower), the remains of which can still be seen. I ventured down to the sweep of sand just below the ruins. At the top of the beach, a yellow glimmering sparkled in the sunlight. It was the emerging blooms of biting stonecrop, a dwarf succulent, with tiny bright green fleshy oval leaves, that are designed to minimise water loss in this well-drained sandy environment. The leaves have a peppery taste, which has led to the alternative name for the plant of wall pepper.

With each passing day during my week-long stay in Harris, my passion for the area grew with increasing intensity, like a rollercoaster love affair in which emotions are hard to control. As well as the spectacular beaches, I explored the mountains of North Harris, including a walk up the picturesque Gleann Mhiabhaig on the Huisinish Road in search of eagles. No eagles materialised, but on Loch Scourst further up the glen, the water was brought to life by a mother black-throated diver and her two well-grown, brown plumaged, youngsters. Families of wheatears flitted in among the rocks and a lone cuckoo called from a distant hill, a last uttering before heading back to its African wintering grounds.

Roseroot (Harris)

On my last day, I headed once more out to the rocky promontory at the head of Loch Chliuthair and sat on a schist-glittered rock slab in the hope of spotting another sea eagle. Rabbits scurried from under my feet on my approach, and I imagine they must be a staple food item of eagles on Harris. As I gazed out to sea, gannets plunge-dived into the Minch for mackerel and gulls swept past on wind-tossed wings. In a rock crevice above me, a roseroot plant had gained fragile hold. Like the biting stonecrop I had discovered earlier in the week on the beach at Rubh' an Teampaill, roseroot has waxy, succulent leaves to prevent desiccation in its specialised rock-crack environment. It was ironic, I pondered, that in this land of heavy and persistent rainfall, many plants had adapted to live in places where water loss was a perennial problem.

I sat for more than an hour. Eventually, it was time to go and, as I reluctantly rose to my feet, a surge of emotion swept upon me, for the wild allure of Harris had consumed my heart in a way I would not have thought possible. As I rounded a rocky spur, a rabbit dashed away, its white-fluffed tail flashing in the late afternoon light. I turned around for one last look at the sea. The gannets were still diving for mackerel and the gulls were still wheeling above the waves.

Chapter 21

SPEEDY SLOW WORMS, TREMBLING ASPENS AND SILVER-GILDED SANDEELS

July 2021 – Sutherland

If there is one thing guaranteed to set my pulse racing while walking in the countryside, it is stumbling upon a piece of corrugated iron dumped on the ground. A bizarre thing to say, perhaps, given it is a form of pollution, but beneath its protective cover, I know from experience, there is every chance some incredible creatures will be lurking.

As I explored the north bankside of the River Kirkaig, near Lochinver in Assynt, Sutherland, searching for butterflies and dragonflies, a large sheet of corrugated iron lying adjacent to an old and crumbled drystane dyke shone-out at me like an irresistible invite. When I was still a teenager, lifting such sheets often revealed field voles, which scuttled away at great speed in brown-furred flashes. Although one of our commonest mammals, field voles are seldom seen; corrugated iron brought an opportunity to see these attractive small rodents close up.

Thus, it was with great anticipation that I gently lifted this sheet of iron abandoned in the wilds of Assynt to reveal a bronze glimmering on the ground beneath – slow worms! There were two of them, intertwined. For a short moment they lay still, then, on realisation that potential danger threatened, they quickly retreated into their narrow underground burrows. I suspect that on sunny days it can get rather hot under this sheet of corrugated iron, and at such times these slow worms will rest within their shallow burrows, but when the weather is cooler, they will reside on the soil surface immediately under the metal, which acts like a thermal mass to deliver warmth.

It was a thrilling find, especially since slow worms are elusive animals and rarely encountered. They are strange creatures – neither worm nor snake, but in fact a legless lizard. Unlike a snake, a slow worm has eyelids and blinks like a lizard. Their internal anatomy shows traces of times long past where legs were present and before evolution took its ultimate course.

If seized roughly a slow worm will shed its tail in the same manner as a lizard. Indeed, its scientific name, *Anguis fragilis* (fragile snake), reflects this likelihood of the tail departing from the body.

Slow Worm

Slow worms are most active after dusk when they leave their shelters and seek out slugs and other invertebrates to feast upon. Somewhat confusingly, slow worms are also known as blind worms. I'm not sure why as their eyes are apparent. Possibly it is because they are often found under rocks and logs where it is perpetually dark. What is undeniable is that their similarity to snakes has led to them having a stained reputation. In Shakespeare's *Macbeth*, for example, the Three Witches added 'blind-worm's sting' to their noxious brew. Slow worms are neither venomous nor do they sting — too often legend and myth unfairly tarnish a creature.

Just as perplexing is the name. The slow worm is not particularly lethargic and can be fast moving when the inclination takes it, although certainly not as fast as a snake. The most likely derivation comes from an old English designation meaning slow snake. Whether such an explanation would satisfy the early twentieth-century naturalist, Edward Step, is quite another matter. In his book *Animal Life of the British Isles* (1921), Step was quite indignant about the nomenclature of the slow worm: '...when it begins to move we are astounded that it has been able to keep such a ridiculous name'.

As intriguing as the pair of slow worms beneath the corrugated iron, was a multitude of black ants that scurried in a fevered manner, the workers carrying the nest's pupae, which were housed in creamy-white cocoons. Before the pupal stage, the workers lick and turn the eggs and feed the larvae on sugars and liquefied insects. In the far corner, a warty brown toad had hunkered down, but unlike the slow worms, it had no intention of moving.

I slowly laid the sheet back on the ground so as to leave the creatures in peace. I sat for a while on top of the drystane dyke to listen to the nearby river and see if any birds might materialise in the surrounding birches. It was a wonderful tonic to spend time in Assynt. This part of the far north west of Scotland I have come to know well. It is easy to become consumed by its magnificent landscape and abundant wildlife, which includes sea eagles and golden eagles.

Sutherland is probably most widely regarded as a wild and empty place of mountains, hills, moors and boggy flows. Yet, it is home to an abundance of rich oases where wildflowers shine and insects buzz. One such oasis is that spot where I stood by the River Kirkaig. Around me, the grass and ferns grew thick, and dark-green fritillary and common blue butterflies flitted past on flashing wings. The common blue is an especially attractive butterfly. As one came to rest on a fern, the azure colour of the top-wings dazzled with the same shimmering intensity as the sky above. The wings then closed and were held upright over the back, displaying the most exquisite patterning of blue, beige and russet, peppered with a sprinkling of dark spots. It is natural perfection.

Despite the name, these little butterflies are far from common, and are localised in their distribution, usually being found near their favoured food plant, bird's-foot trefoil. Common blues are fickle and even in areas where bird's-foot trefoil grows in abundance they can be completely absent. I am intrigued by such distribution anomalies where a creature is missing from a habitat which otherwise looks ideal for them. All sorts of unseen environmental factors can be at work, but for much of the time, I suspect it is just down to chance.

A fascinating aspect of common blue ecology is that their caterpillars have forged a unique relationship with ants. In an arrangement of 'you scratch my back, and I'll scratch yours', the caterpillars secrete nutrient-containing substances that the ants feed upon, while at the same time, the ants protect the butterfly larvae from predators. The capacity of nature to innovate and evolve is a continual source of wonderment to me.

I rose from my resting place and headed further up the river, where lay a series of rocky pools and runs, following a tranquil wooded gorge where hazel, birch and aspen abound and on towards the spectacular Falls of Kirkaig. Aspen is a tree that forever holds me under its thrall, for when the wind blows something quite remarkable happens: the leaves begin to tremble and quiver in delightful fashion. The scientific name, *Populus tremula*, means trembling poplar and to sit by one and listen to the wind rustling through the leaves is a wonderful experience.

The early twentieth-century poet, Edward Thomas, eloquently wrote of how the 'the whisper of the aspens' could not even be subdued by the 'ringing of hammer' and the 'clink and hum' emanating from a local blacksmith. Folklore states that this trembling of the leaves was an indication of a secret guilt – most likely because it was believed to be the wood used to make the cross on which Christ was crucified. One book I came across on Celtic traditions – *Every Earthly Blessing* by Esther de Waal (1999) – claimed the 'aspen tree was particularly loathed' because it 'had haughtily held up its head while all the others in the forest had bowed down, proud that it had been chosen by the enemies of Christ as the wood for the cross'.

The leaf stalks of the aspen are long and flattened, a combination that makes the leaves flutter easily in a breeze. In autumn, when its leaves are turning in hue, the sight of a trembling aspen is one to inspire. Another interesting tale proffers that a crown made of aspen leaves gives the wearer the power to visit and safely return from the Underworld. Aspen crowns have even been found in ancient burial mounds to allow the spirits of the deceased to be reborn. The aspen's Greek name, aspis, means shield and, unsurprisingly, the wood was a much-favoured material for their manufacture in ancient times.

Above the Falls of Kirkaig, the woodland petered out and a spectacular landscape unfolded before my eyes, including the dramatic double-peaked hulk of Suilven, as well as the high tops of Canisp, Stac Pollaidh and Ben More Assynt. I had climbed Suilven the previous year from Glencanisp, a long seven-and-a-half-hour return hike, which is well worth the effort for the staggering views afforded from the summit, overlooking a majestic landscape of hill, loch and moor.

Falls of Kirkaig, and Aspen

Soon, I reached the shore of Fionn Loch and a small gravelly beach, which provided the perfect rest stop for lunch. Tranquil, peat-stained coppery water lapped the shore, and with the backdrop of Suilven, it was hard to imagine a more beautiful spot in the whole of Scotland. Fionn Loch is a part of a complex body of water that stretches like a probing finger all the way to the village of Elphin some 11km further east by connecting into Loch Veyatie through the narrow watery channel of Uid Fhearna.

As I neared the end of my lunch, a greyish wader with trailing legs soared above me, and spiralled away over a distant peaty, heather-clad hummock. It was a greenshank, its appearance so tantalisingly brief, yet one that stirred my emotions with real excitement.

Greenshanks are such special birds. They so enthralled the eminent Scottish-based ornithologist, Desmond Nethersole-Thompson, that he described the species as 'the most wonderful bird that flies'. He first studied them on their breeding grounds in the north of Scotland in 1932 and soon became a complete greenshank addict, a bird he freely admitted to having fallen in love with. He described the spectacular aerial courtship of the males as 'song-dances', a description that evocatively portrays the true splendour of their breeding displays.

In his book *Highland Birds* (1971), Nethersole-Thompson wrote:

> *What a dramatic song flight the cock greenshank has. High in the air, sometimes in the clouds, a small dark gnat-like thing soars and switchbacks, and all the time he sings his wild ecstatic song.*

With the greenshank gone, I examined the backshore behind me, my attention having been drawn by a striking common blue damselfly. I also discovered a large mayfly resting on the stem of a rush. It was a green drake mayfly, which seemed to be in a state of semi-torpor, providing the ideal opportunity for closer examination. This is a large species of mayfly, and the intricate venation on its semi-transparent wings was spellbinding, having a regularity of arrangement that could have been designed by an architect. Mayflies are an ecological keystone of lochs, rivers and burns, their larvae or nymphs forming crucial food for trout – a larder of protein on the waterbed. Females, when laying eggs in the water are, also eagerly snapped up by fish, as are the spent adults, which die not long after mating.

On my return journey, I repeatedly scanned the skyline on either side of the glen for eagles, a habit borne from a lifetime of walking the hills. The ridgetops remained empty, but there was plenty of other interest, including fragrant orchids adorning the path edges, and speckled wood butterflies twirling in the woodland margins. Soon, I was back down at Loch Kirkaig where the river tumbled out into the sea. It is interesting comparing the differences between estuaries on the east coast and those in the North West Highlands. East coast ones – the River Eden in Fife being a good example – are often large complex affairs with sandbars and mud banks and substantial areas of shallow water. Those in the north west typically rush down to the sea through the rocky landscape and quickly empty into the ocean like a gushing drainpipe; no elaborate channels or intricate bays, just straight into the sea and that's that.

Suilven & Butterflies
L-R: Speckled Wood; Six Spot Burnet (background); Scotch Argus; Meadow Brown

The following day, I headed north to just beyond the hamlet of Kylesku, and took the track on the north side of Loch Gleann Dubh. The weather gods were smiling once more, and it was a glorious sunny day, the high tops of Quinag providing an imposing backdrop to the south-west. The startling flowers of yellow saxifrage gleamed from exposed cuts by the track edge, Scotch argus and meadow brown butterflies danced in the light breeze, while harbour seals porpoised playfully out on the water. There were also numerous golden-ringed dragonflies, which have impressive 10cm wingspans. One female frequently stabbed her banded tail into the shallow still waters of an adjacent drainage ditch to deposit her eggs. These eggs will soon hatch into underwater nymphs (larvae) – a stage which they remain in for two to five years, after which time, the nymphs will transform into the most beautiful dragonflies and the wheel of life will have turned full circle once more.

Another highlight of my visit to Sutherland was an excursion to Sandwood Bay in the far north west, close to Cape Wrath. More than 200 different species of plants, including eight orchids, prosper on the machair here. On the 7 km long walk-in to Sandwood Bay, a vast peaty landscape unfolded, providing home for a variety of creatures and plants that have adapted to live in this acidic, waterlogged landscape. Here, plants such as bog asphodel bloomed in profusion with their attractive yellow flower-spikes, and carpets of lilac-hued wild thyme gleamed on the drier, well-drained peat banks.

Sandwood Bay is an enchanting place, a broad sweep of glinting sand, bordered by rugged cliffs and the imposing sea stack of Am Buachaille (The Shepherd), along with several rocky islets which, I imagine, must teem with undersea life. Equally intriguing is the large, shifting sand-dune system that backs onto the bay, where I encountered several six-spot burnet moths flying haphazardly in among the marram grass. Their glossy black forewings, spotted with crimson, flashed and glowed in an engaging fashion as they fluttered over the dunes in short flights.

Despite the tranquil surroundings, folklore holds that the beach is home to a group of doomed ghostly sailors, shipwrecked long before a lighthouse was built in the early nineteenth century. It is certainly likely that Viking longships would have stopped here as they made their way past Cape Wrath on their trade routes between Scotland and Scandinavia.

As I sat on the beach looking out at the crashing, white-frothed rollers, I noticed a couple of knots on the sand just above the highest water margin, still resplendent in their colourful brick-red breeding plumage. It was only early July but already these waders had returned from their breeding grounds in Greenland and Arctic Canada, perhaps having just made their first landfall in this far north west tip of Scotland only hours previously. Tired after such a long migration, Sandwood Bay would have been a welcome sight as they swept in from low over the sea. Due to their early arrival, I suspect they were failed breeders, and the eagerness in which they probed the sand for invertebrates was a clear sign of their hunger and the need to gain sustenance.

On another occasion during my visit to Sutherland, this time in Assynt near Lochinver, a pine marten bounded across a small road in front of my car, and paused for a while to snuffle in the grass by the verge. It was a sublimely attractive beast with a rich dark brown coat finished off with a creamy yellow bib and a long bushy tail. The early twentieth-century naturalist, Frances Pitt, was so taken by the pine marten that she wrote:

> *Imagine it as remarkably graceful and nimble, with an*
> *expression of intelligent curiosity, and you will have some*
> *idea of a most beautiful being.*

Until the nineteenth century pine martens were widespread in Scotland, but relentless persecution and high demand for their luxuriant soft pelts soon saw the population plummet. Records from one estate near Glen Feshie in the Cairngorms reveal that 246 pine martens were despatched between 1837 and 1840 alone.

Such enthusiasm amongst landowners to rid their land of pine martens was probably in the most part misplaced, for rather than being an avid devourer of game their diet comprises principally voles, mice, rabbits, small birds, insects, berries and fungi.

By the early 1900s the pine marten was only holding out in remote areas of the north west Highlands. Since the Second World War there has been a remarkable turnaround in their fortunes, with afforestation and a more enlightened attitude to their presence helping to fuel a quite remarkable recovery. Pine martens now occur throughout much of Scotland, and in my home county of Clackmannanshire I often stumble upon their signs when out walking.

On my final day in Sutherland, the underwater lure of Loch Kirkaig became overpowering, especially since the sun still maintained its hold in what had transpired to be an unusually long settled spell. I have a love-hate relationship with Loch Kirkaig when snorkelling. On the positive side, it has thrown up before my eyes a host of unusual sea creatures over the years, including poisonous lesser weever fish and mysterious pipefish, which are related to seahorses. The downside is that the freshwater that flows into this sea loch from the River Kirkaig results in the underwater visibility often becoming blurry. Water of different salinities form distinct layers, a bit like olive oil on vinegar, and when the two layers are mixed, such as by the movement of a snorkeller, the visibility diminishes into a strange, unfocused world. The interface between these layers is termed a halocline.

I have lost count of the number of times in Loch Kirkaig when I have brought my underwater camera to bear upon a fish or other sea creature, only for the water to turn almost opaque due to my movements disturbing the halocline. If I were to stop swimming and hang motionless in the water, the visibility would quickly become sparkling clear once more.

For this reason, when visiting Assynt, I usually snorkel in those bays and sea lochs located further north. Nonetheless, I plunged into Loch Kirkaig and was soon immersed within its ethereal beauty of seaweed forests and open exposed areas of mud and sand. There was life everywhere, most notably numerous green shore crabs, which are of fundamental importance to our inshore marine environment, a double act of being vital seabed scavengers while also being food for so many other creatures. Larger fish such as cod will prey upon these crabs when they have moulted and are in their temporary soft-shelled stage – peelers as they are known. Juvenile crabs, as planktonic larvae, are avidly devoured by small fish. There was a fair bit of squabbling going on among these crabs, and as I glided over the seabed, several squared up to one another.

The shallowest parts of the loch were unusually warm from the sunshine, and it was a pleasant experience pottering about in such areas, searching for smaller marine creatures. Among the most numerous were tiny semi-transparent mysid shrimps with long proboscises and hump-back bodies, which are sometimes known as opossum shrimps.

Like crab larvae, they are eaten by numerous creatures. In effect, I was swimming through an underwater food factory – a nursery area for fish and other animals, and the reason why inshore waters are so important to such a wide variety of marine creatures. I kicked my flippers several more times and headed out away from the shore and into water about 2m deep. A silvery cloud swept past my face mask – lesser sandeels – hundreds of them, a huge glittering shoal.

I followed the sandeels, which sometimes disappeared in the haze created by the disturbed halocline, but then miraculously appeared again. These sandeels were astounding to watch, a vast silvery conglomeration of glistening life, which out of curiosity often swerved close by me, their flanks glinting under the sunshine from the sky above.

Sandeels are the bread-and-butter sustenance for many sea creatures, providing an oil-rich, nutritious food source avidly devoured by seabirds and fish such as mackerel. I followed the sandeels for a while longer, completely entranced by the perfect synchronisation of their movement. They swung past me once more, before suddenly disappearing into a blur of impenetrable water – the halocline had reared its ugly head once more. The water soon cleared, but this time there was no more sign of their silver-gilded forms – the sandeels had disappeared.

As I slowly made my way back to shore, watching crabs scuttle below me, little was I to know that the importance of sandeels to the marine environment would soon be brought forcefully home to me on the final leg of my wildlife odyssey to the far-flung northern isles of Shetland.

Chapter 22

BONXIES, TAMMIE NORRIES, TIRRICKS AND A SKYLARK SWANSONG

July 2021 – Shetland

A mass of gannets on open wings spiralled in the air above me, accompanied by a clamouring cacophony drawn from the heart of nature – a wild calling of the ocean, so entrancing that I yearned to become more deeply immersed within its warm embrace.

The towering cliffs of the Isle of Noss in east Shetland brought a shadow over the sea and there were seabirds everywhere: gannets, guillemots, razorbills and fulmars, all with an air of urgency as they shuttled back and forth to their nesting ledges where rapidly growing down-fluffed youngsters sat on impossibly narrow rock ledges.

These magnificent cliffs cradled the dawn of new life, yet death was all around too, and near our Shetland Seabird Tours' boat, a bonxie swam around the body of a young gannet that had fallen into the sea from its precarious ledge, pecking and stabbing upon the remains with its formidable hook-tipped beak. Life can be so cruel and short. If this youngster had not had the misfortune to fall, probably as the result of a squabble with another gannet, it could have looked forward to a long life, perhaps of up to 40 years.

Also known as the great skua, the bonxie is the supreme aerial sea predator, pirate and scavenger, prowling the cliff margins on fast-beating wings, forever on the lookout for unguarded chicks. This was a time of rich bounty for bonxies because each cliff ledge held a potential meal. The prolificacy of the feeding available was illustrated by the bonxie feeding upon the floating body of the young gannet, for many other bonxies swooped low overhead, yet showed no interest in joining the feast.

The result of the marauding bonxies was plain to see on other parts of the cliff faces, and by the fringes of one large sea cave, a small nesting cluster of kittiwakes had taken such a toll from the bonxies and great-black backed gulls that now only a handful of nests still held young. Bonxies, kittiwakes and other seabirds have coexisted in balanced harmony since the dawn of time. Today, more insidious forces are at work, driving a decline in kittiwakes and many other seabirds due a dearth of sandeels to feed upon – the very fish that had enthralled me so recently in a Sutherland sea loch. At Noss, which means nose in old Norse, breeding numbers of kittiwakes have catastrophically plummeted by over 90 per cent over the last two decades, and UK-wide kittiwake numbers have fallen by half since the 1960s.

The underlying problem is related to Britain's warming seas, which has led to planktonic ecosystem shifts resulting in a decline in the abundance and size of sandeels. Kittiwakes are especially vulnerable to food shortages as they can only take prey such as sandeels, sprats and juvenile herring when they occur at or near the surface of the sea, unlike deeper diving species such as gannets, guillemots and razorbills which have access to a greater variety of prey in the water column. It is a vicious circle. As kittiwake nesting colonies get smaller due to lack of food, they become even more liable to predation by bonxies and gulls because there are fewer adults about to defend their nests as a large protective group.

Sandeel populations were initially depleted by industrial fishing. Following a local, chronic stock decline, this practice ceased around Shetland in 2003 to enable stocks to recover. There is currently no UK commercial interest in sandeel fishing. Fishing by Danish, Norwegian and Swedish boats, however, continue in other parts of the North Sea – for fish meal and fish oil for agricultural and aquaculture feed production – including the Dogger Bank and areas off the Firth of Forth just outside a closed sandeel fishing area or 'box' that was imposed over 20 years ago to protect stocks.

While climate change may currently be the main driver affecting sandeel populations, the plight of the kittiwake means that the continuation of the industrial sandeel fishery is madness in the extreme, serving to make a bad situation even worse. With the UK now an independent coastal state following Brexit, with its own exclusive economic zone, ambition needs to be adopted to prohibit or dramatically curtail commercial sandeel fishing in Scottish and UK waters. The future of our kittiwakes, and other species affected, such as Arctic skuas and terns, depends upon such decisive action.

As our boat made its way along the foot of the Noss seabird cliffs, other threats to seabirds became only too apparent. Many of the gannet nests were adorned with discarded fishing rope and netting, which the birds were using as nesting material, a stark reminder of the plastic pollution that pervades our oceans.

Gannets (Noss, Shetland)

Precariousness hung over the imposing sea cliffs at Noss like a brooding cloud. For the moment, I shrugged such dark thoughts aside, buoyed by the throngs of seabirds, wheeling in the cool northern sea air above me, their joyous wings bringing hope over this sea of uncertainty. Noss, with its soaring cliffs that reach a height of 180 m, is home to around 25,000 breeding gannets, and the sky was full of their sharp-winged forms. Gannets take about four to five years to develop into sexually mature adults, and on many of the lower guano-covered rock shelves by the sea edge adolescent birds had gathered, hanging around like unruly teenagers, socialising – and bickering – with one another. Pair bonds will start to develop at such times and the act of being in amongst this vast colony will be a huge learning experience for the youngsters as they observe the frenzied activity of the adults around them. The best cliff ledges are at a premium, and I wondered if these young gannets were absorbing such information in their minds as a precursor for their first nesting attempts.

Lying on the same latitude as the southern tip of Greenland, the National Nature Reserve of Noss is one of the most important seabird colonies in the North Atlantic. Gannets are large seabirds, and the attraction of the Noss cliffs lies in the power of erosion, which has weathered hard and soft layers of rock at different rates to form tier upon tier of broad ledges that provide perfect nesting sites. Such was the depth of each tier, many of them were effectively roofed by the one above, providing extra protection.

The Great Skua, also known as the Bonxie

The bonxies were fascinating to watch. As our boat approached Noss, they followed its course in the hope of being tossed a herring or two, which were being kept aside to throw to the gannets later in the trip so that the tour passengers could witness their spectacular plunges into the water from close range. The bonxie is by nature a sea pirate, robbing other seabirds of their valuable catches of fish, and even those as large as gannets are actively sought out. Around the cliffs of a breeding seabird colony, a bonxie will latch onto the tail of a flying kittiwake or guillemot and give chase with such tenacious ferocity that the unfortunate bird is forced to disgorge its stomach contents, which the bonxie will swoop down to catch. As well as taking seabird chicks, bonxies will directly prey upon smaller seabirds such as puffins by plucking them straight out of the air. On nearby shores and areas of moorland they will search out the eggs and young of eider ducks and waders. Bonxies will eat anything they can get their beaks on; fish and other marine creatures are also devoured, underlining their versatility in exploiting every possible food source available. The name bonxie is possibly derived from an old Norse word meaning dumpy, which is a direct reflection of its heavy-set build.

Shetland is an extraordinary place, a narrowly aligned, yet sprawling archipelago stretching from Fair Isle in the south to Unst in the north. As I explored the islands, panoramas of the east coast and west coast and their deep, narrow voes, alternated like a hypnotic pendulum. Although closer to mainland Scotland than Norway, the Norse influence on Shetland is all pervading. It is steeped into the islands' soul, which is indicated by its place names, such as wick (bay or inlet), voe (creek) and ness (headland).

The long, convoluted coastline comprising voes and firths, numerous islands, islets and skerries, along with imposing cliffs and headlands, and secluded sandy beaches lapped by a rich ocean, are all hallmarks of Shetland's inspiring land and seascape, which is brought under focus by an ever-changing kaleidoscope of reflective light. The diversity of the weather changes is even more remarkable than on the Scottish mainland, with rain one moment, sun the next, then creeping mists taking hold and lifting again. For what on the map looks a small place, in the actuality it is much bigger than the mind first envisages, and one could spend a lifetime exploring these islands and still not discover all its natural secrets. I was smitten by Shetland from my first visit over three decades ago and, ever since, my affection has grown into a deep and burning passion that gains in intensity with each passing year.

One place that excites is Sumburgh Head on the southern tip of mainland Shetland. The stars are the puffins, and twice during my six-day stay in the islands, I was drawn by the allure of getting up close to these comical little auks. It is fascinating how some creatures inspire like few others and are universally adored. The robin and red squirrel are obvious examples, as is the puffin, a wonderful chunky little seabird with its black and white dinner suit plumage and large multicoloured bill.

Puffins nest in burrows on the top of cliffs and on adjacent steep grassy slopes, meaning the topography at Sumburgh Head is perfect for their requirements. In addition, the sizeable rabbit population on Sumburgh's clifftops provides another advantage. Although puffins are more than capable of making their own burrows by using their bill and feet to push the soil out behind them, they frequently use redundant rabbit burrows, which saves time and effort in construction. It is easy to overlook the Sumburgh rabbits such is the attraction of the puffins, but they live most interesting lifestyles, often grazing on frighteningly steep slopes that run down in between cliff buttresses. Like the young seabirds, baby rabbits run the continual gauntlet of bonxies and gulls and need to be perpetually alert.

Almost as addictive as watching the puffins was observing the reaction of tourists enjoying being in proximity to them. Their obvious pleasure was evident from the smiling faces of both children and adults alike and underlined more than ever our close bond and connection with nature. We are as one, living in the same world and dependent upon a healthy environment for our future wellbeing. Sadly, like the kittiwake, puffin numbers around Shetland are in freefall, a testimony to the failure of humanity to act and bring about urgent change.

Orca (Shetland Waters)

I was especially keen to spot orcas during my stay in Shetland so scoured the voes from north to south and east to west, the unusually calm waters offering the perfect conditions for spotting their distinctive large dorsal fins breaking the water. Two semi-resident pods regularly hunt close inshore for seals, however, the sea area they cover is vast, and the orcas remained elusive, and my quest proved fruitless, as it has done on every previous visit. Shetland waters are home to a variety of other cetaceans, including Risso's dolphins and Atlantic white-sided dolphins.

Arctic Tern & Chick

Despite the lack of orcas, exploring the wild coastline was uplifting and wherever I went the constant calls of Arctic terns filled the air. In Shetland, Arctic terns are known as tirricks in reflection of their distinctive omnipresent calls. On one remote pebbly beach in west Shetland, a young tirrick, a downy little grey bundle, suddenly scurried ahead of me before squeezing itself against a rock, into which it pressed its face to avoid eye contact. It lay huddled, stony still, not even daring to peek at me. I wondered what was going through its mind. Relying on camouflage was its last line of defence and it would have been a nerve-racking moment, unsure whether I was friend or foe and whether it was on the verge of meeting an untimely end. I quickly retreated to leave the youngster alone, so it could relax once more and lest a bonxie should become aware of its whereabouts. Such is the ubiquitous nature of Arctic terns in Shetland, I imagine local people find it a sad moment when the birds depart in late summer, and an occasion of real joy when they return in May, just like the first arrivals of swallows instil in other parts of the country. Indeed, it is more than apparent that since the earliest of times Shetlanders have had a particularly close affinity with nature, and this is reflected in the wide variety of local names for creatures, such as tirrick. Puffins are known as tammie norries and black guillemots as tysties. The alternative name, bonxie, for the great skua hails from Shetland too, and is the preferred and most widely-used option for many people, including myself.

A friend of mine was lucky enough to have discovered a moulting, red-necked phalarope on Loch of Clumlie in south Shetland the week before my arrival, so I ventured there one afternoon in the hope it might still be there. Red-necked phalaropes are enigmas – diminutive waders that breed on freshwater pools and mires in the Arctic and sub-Arctic. Shetland lies towards the southern limit of their breeding range and a few pairs nest on the island of Fetlar each summer. Like the dotterel, which I went in search of in the Cairngorms the previous month, the red-necked phalarope exhibits a curious sexual role reversal where once the female has laid her eggs, the male will take over the incubation and look after the young, while the female uses her brightly-coloured plumage to attract new partners.

Only recently, through the use of tiny geolocator tags, it has come to light that Fetlar's phalaropes make an epic 25,000 km round trip during their migration, spending the winter off the coast of Ecuador and Peru, where the plankton-rich waters delivered by the Humboldt Current provide bountiful feeding. Interestingly, phalaropes that breed in nearby Scandinavia migrate to the Arabian Sea to spend the winter. It is now known that those phalaropes that breed in Scotland, Greenland and Iceland belong to a distinct and separate population, which winters in the Pacific. How did such differences evolve – two populations almost within touching distance of one another in summer, yet with such different migration routes, and a vast separation during winter? In another intriguing evolutionary twist, the wings of red-necked phalaropes breeding in Greenland, Iceland and Scotland are longer than those of birds breeding in Fennoscandia and Russia because of the much larger migratory flights they take.

I scanned the water margins of Loch of Clumlie with my binoculars, but there was no sign of the lone phalarope and it had probably moved on somewhere else, although they are small birds, and it was entirely possible it was still there, yet hidden out of sight. Compensation was brought through the presence of several red-throated divers with their distinctive low profiles gliding across the water by the far edge of the loch. About the size of a small goose, they are attractive birds with their light grey heads and vibrant red throats, although such colour was hard to discern through my binoculars as grey cloud shrouded the sky and the light was flat.

An old Shetland name for the red-throated diver is rain-goose, in reference to the long-held belief that the bird can foretell the bad weather with short cries (or flying inland) indicating fine weather, while long, plaintive ones (or flying out to sea) give a warning of more inclement conditions. A sceptic might suggest such meteorological forecasting skills were bound to bear fruit, given that the weather in Shetland is rarely settled for any length of time.

John Spence, writing on weather lore and quoting an old Shetland poem in his *Shetland Folk-lore* (1899), explained:

> *The flight of the rain goose (the red-throated diver) was particularly noticed. When this bird was seen flying in an inland direction the weather was likely to be favourable, but when its flight was directed towards the sea the opposite was expected. Hence – "If the rain gose flees ta da hill, Ye can geng ta da haf whin ye will; Bit whin sho gengs ta da sea. Ye maun draw up yir boats an flee".*

Everywhere I travelled in Shetland brought new surprises and the most absorbing scenery. The cliffs at Eshaness in the north west and those at Deepdale further south were eye-catching for their sheer immensity and drama. At Deepdale, several mountain hares scurried on the clifftops. Along with the rabbit, the hare is one of the few land mammals to occur on Shetland. The rocky cove at Westerwick in the west held special appeal to me due to its enchanting setting, which could almost have been cast from a film set.

I was also much taken by the No Ness peninsula on the south east mainland, which unveiled a spectacular panorama down the coast to Sumburgh Head. Here, a pair of Arctic skuas swept low over my head. Smaller, less common, and more graceful in form than the bonxie, they too are birds with an uncertain future. Like the bonxie, Arctic skuas dive-bomb other seabirds to force them to disgorge or release their fish catch. At one time, it was erroneously believed that Arctic skuas dive-bombed other birds to persuade them to defecate, which has led to several old common names that include dirt bird and dirty Allan. In Shetland, they are known as scooty Allans.

Wherever I went, breeding whimbrels were sometimes glimpsed, which reminded me of my earlier encounter with these long-billed curlew-like waders at Loch Linnhe as they migrated up the Scottish west coast to their northern nesting grounds. The lack of large birds of prey such as buzzards and eagles was a noticeable feature of the Shetland landscape compared to the rest of Scotland, but in this instance their niche has been filled to a degree by the bonxies. There is, however, the exciting prospect that sea eagles will soon recolonise Shetland after the last bird in the islands was hunted to extinction in 1918.

On my final day, I ventured to Unst, the northernmost isle in the Shetland archipelago, passing through Yell on the way. Unst is a northern jewel with several sweeps of fine sandy beaches, dramatic cliffs, bays and voes. Hermaness Nature Reserve on the far northern tip was a place I had not been to before, and it drew me in like an irresistible magnet, somewhere that I instinctively knew my feet had to tread so that my lungs could breathe in the essence of the wild north.

It wasn't the ideal day to visit Hermaness, as low cloud and mist swirled across the moorland approach walk. In a strange way that didn't matter, and the grey murk accentuated the wildness and remoteness of this far northern fringe of Scotland. White-fluffed bog cotton nodded in the breeze and the small yellow blooms of tormentil dotted the ground, while bonxies floated in and out of the wisp as they patrolled the air. Hermaness, or Herma's Headland, is named after a mythical giant who fought with a neighbouring giant, Saxa, over a beautiful mermaid. They tossed enormous boulders at each other over the Burra Firth, one of which landed in the sea and became Out Stack, a rocky outcrop, which today is Britain's most northerly point.

This was a place of myth and legend, and as I approached the clifftop, the calls of gannets, guillemots and razorbills spirited up through the air. Hermaness is home to over 100,000 breeding seabirds, yet as I peered over the cliff edge none could be seen because of the grey, opaque mist. I could, nonetheless, smell them, the rich pungent odour of guano upwelling in the air currents, and their cries from down below were the essence of nature's wild beating heart. The mist momentarily lifted to reveal a rocky islet in the sea below, where a mass of nesting gannets had congregated on a sloping shelf. The mist swirled in again with the suddenness of a closing theatre curtain, and the gannet rock disappeared into the grey void. The show was over.

Behind me, a skylark piped up, a short end-of-season warble, and a pale shadow of the glorious song these birds rain down upon our hills, fields and saltmarshes in spring. How appropriate I thought, for it was a skylark that had first greeted me on a cold, frost-glinted morning on the merse at Caerlaverock in Dumfriesshire back in March at the start of my journey, and which now had delivered the swansong to my Scottish wildlife odyssey. My emotions surprised and confused me in equal measure. I had expected sadness at reaching journey's end, but all I could feel was exultant joy, a surge of euphoria at the wondrous nature this small country on the wild Atlantic edge had thrown before me, and my soul clamoured for more, a pulsing surge that I knew would be impossible to quench.

EPILOGUE

A couple of weeks after I had finished writing *A Scottish Wildlife Odyssey*, a landmark report on climate change was published by the UN. The report resonated with me immediately because I had so recently seen the impact of climate change on Shetland's kittiwakes and other seabirds.

The Intergovernmental Panel on Climate Change's Sixth Assessment Report made grim reading with UN Secretary-General Antonio Guterres describing the report's warning as a 'code red for humanity'. He cautioned that the world must 'wake up' and act on climate change following the report which stated that a target of limiting global warming to 1.5°c will be breached within two decades.

Reading the main headlines from the report was depressing, and it also brought about an irresistible urge for me to revisit an area of Scotland most likely to be affected by climate change – the montane plateaux of the Cairngorms, which is home to so many specialist arctic-alpine creatures. They are like wild refugees in an isolated upland landscape, and if climate change continues apace, they will potentially have nowhere left to go. In particular, I had a strong urge to see once more snow buntings in their breeding haunts in the high Cairngorm corries. Snow buntings are sparrow-sized birds and in summer the male has a wonderful contrasting black and white plumage, while the female is more muted in tone, but attractive nonetheless. They are rare breeding birds in Scotland – around 50 pairs – and their days could well be numbered here because Scotland is a southern outpost; their main breeding range being Iceland, Greenland and Scandinavia.

So, a few days after the report was published, I set out one dawn to ascend Cairn Lochan and then onto Ben Macdui, Scotland's second highest mountain. Many years ago, I used to watch snow buntings in the boulder fields that flank Ben Macdui and I fervently hoped once more to witness these eye-catching birds whirling through the air like dancing snowflakes.

It was a wonderful morning to be in the Cairngorms. The wind blew strong and the cloud rose and fell like an undulating grey shroud, sometimes enveloping the highest tops, then lifting, so that I could see mountains and hills in the distance, including Lochnagar, and as far away as Bennachie near Inverurie in Aberdeenshire.

Through the thick grey soup of cloud I reached the top of Ben Macdui, before descending a short distance down the western flank which overlooks the Lairig Ghru, an imposing mountain pass that cuts through the heart of the Cairngorms. The mist lifted once more, and on the far side of the Lairig Ghru, the high tops of Sgòr an Lochain Uaine, Einich Cairn and Braeriach momentarily appeared, the clouds spiralling in thin grey wispy tendrils around their high corries. Seconds later, the cloud came down again so that once more I was immersed in a blanket of grey.

I scoured the boulder fields and steep open flanks of Ben Macdui, especially areas fringing moss and montane grasses, but never caught a glimpse of any snow buntings. They were there, of that I was certain, but in this vast area, finding them was like searching for a needle in a haystack. While there were no birds about, my eyes were continually drawn to club mosses and lime-green lichens that encrusted the rocks and boulders in this wild, cold and inhospitable place. It was a strangely compelling environment, a place that ensnares you by its wild emptiness and one that makes you feel exceedingly small.

On the return trek, there was plenty of time to reflect upon my Scottish wildlife journey and the bountiful nature this small country on the wild north Atlantic edge holds. Scotland is special, of that there is no doubt, and the richness of its nature held me in its thrall from the beginning at Caerlaverock to the end at Hermaness in Unst. There is much to be joyful and hopeful about, and, of course, there is much to worry us, most notably in climate change. There are all kinds of potential impacts from climate change, including destabilisation of the warming sea current, the North Atlantic Drift, which is showing signs of increasing weakening. Ironically, when all the talk is about increasing temperatures, the diminishment of the North Atlantic Drift, could result in colder weather overall to northern Europe, and cause immense and unpredictable turmoil with global weather systems. There are so many unknowns: warmer or colder, drier or wetter – it is a lottery of uncertainty and upheaval.

As the UN report indicated, we need to change our lifestyles, the way we produce our food, and in particular reduce our dependence on fossil fuels and move to cleaner forms of energy. We also need to look after and enhance our natural environment. I have only dipped briefly into my concerns, about grazing pressure on our uplands, for example, or industrial fishing for sandeels, for the intention of this book is a celebration of Scotland's nature, rather than acting as a platform for change on how we manage our land and oceans. While I have opinions developed over a lifetime of trekking our countryside or diving in our seas, I recognise that there are complexities in many environmental issues that result in things seldom being black or white, and that all views, whatever their flavour, demand credence and respect.

What I am certain about, though, is that trying to find a pathway for change that benefits both humanity and the wider environment can only be resolved through dialogue. Rewilding initiatives, for example, must have everyone on board, especially those in rural communities where economic and environmental considerations must go hand in hand, with one not diminishing the other.

The twentieth-century Scottish naturalist, John Morton Boyd, was a pioneer when it came to having a balanced and pragmatic attitude towards land management and conservation. He became the first regional officer of the Nature Conservancy for the West Highlands and Islands in 1957 and was later appointed its director in Scotland.

In his book, *The Song of the Sandpiper* (1999), he remarked upon the disconnect that sometimes happened between scientists and conservationists with the general rural population, which also ran counter to the aspirations of both local and central government to create jobs and attract people back to depopulated areas.

Referring to the then Nature Conservancy Council (NCC) in the period of the 1980s with regards to the implementation of Sites of Special Scientific Interest, he wrote that some staff, while highly competent in natural science, inevitably lacked the personal and communication skills necessary to deliver the NCC's conservation message, which when interpretated wrongly appeared arrogant and even hostile to local feeling.

* * *

He added:

> *Local people were asked by the NCC to make real sacrifices for esoteric reasons based on a new and unfamiliar culture called 'nature conservation'... It was vital that nature conservation was welcomed by the whole community and that national policies were expressed locally with flexibility and sensitivity.*

There are, without a doubt, still elements of such disconnect that occur today, but in the intervening years there has been a discernible shift in public opinion where there is recognition that a healthy and diverse environment is both desirable and an economic asset with the potential to create jobs if brought about in the right manner.

Such thoughts tumbled through my mind as I skirted round the silvery waters of Lochan Buidhe and then onwards for my final leg to Coire Cas. As I made my way down by the edge of the Cairngorm ski runs, a vibrant yellow cluster of bog asphodel sparkled from a damp flush. I hunkered down to examine the clump and gently brushed my fingers over their intricate flower spikes. They were a shining beacon of hope, each yellow petal carefully crafted by the hand of nature, and when nature draws you deep within its wild embrace, it will never let you go, and in turn, we should cherish nature, and never let it go.

ABOUT THE AUTHOR

Keith Broomfield is a well-known Scottish nature writer who has had a passion for wildlife since childhood.

A graduate in zoology from the University of Aberdeen, Keith's writing covers virtually every element of the natural world from flora and fungi, to invertebrates, mammals, birds and marine life.

He writes a weekly 'Nature Watch' column for *The Courier* and *The Press & Journal* newspapers, as well as his 'On the Wildside' column for the *Alloa Advertiser*, and occasional pieces for *The Scotsman*. Keith is a trustee/director of the Forth Rivers Trust, a board member of *The Forth Naturalist & Historian*, a director of Catch PR Ltd, a committee member of the Devon Angling Association, and a member of the Central Scotland Raptor Study Group.

This is his second book with Tippermuir. His first, *'If Rivers Could Sing': A Scottish River Wildlife Journey. A Year in the Life of the River Devon as it flows through the Counties of Perthshire, Kinross-shire & Clackmannanshire* (2020), has received much acclaim and was shortlisted by the Saltire Society in the Scotland's National Book Awards for 'First Book' of the Year 2021.

IF RIVERS COULD SING:
A SCOTTISH WILDLIFE JOURNEY
Keith Broomfield

SHORTLISTED FOR THE SCOTLAND'S NATIONAL BOOK AWARDS - 'FIRST BOOK' OF THE YEAR 2021

Rivers have captivated wildlife writer Keith Broomfield since childhood: special serene places where nature abounds, and surprises unfold at every turn. In this personal Scottish river wildlife journey, he delves deeper into his own local river to explore its abundant wildlife and to get closer to its beating heart. The course of the Devon is a place Keith has come to know well and somewhere that has become part of his being. It is a place that stirs emotions and brings back eclectic memories: otters playing by a far bank; a streaking flash of electric-blue as a kingfisher whirrs upriver; and the challenge of seeking out elusive beavers in the quieter backwaters.

If Rivers Could Sing is a book for all who love wildlife, wild places, and Scotland's natural heritage.

ISBN 9781913836009 Paperback £9.99

TIPPERMUIR BOOKS

Tippermuir Books Ltd is an independent
publishing company based in Perth, Scotland.

PUBLISHING HISTORY

Spanish Thermopylae (2009)

Battleground Perthshire (2009)

Perth: Street by Street (2012)

Born in Perthshire (2012)

In Spain with Orwell (2013)

Trust (2014)

Perth: As Others Saw Us (2014)

Love All (2016)

A Chocolate Soldier (2016)

The Early Photographers of Perthshire (2016)

Taking Detective Novels Seriously:
The Collected Crime Reviews of Dorothy L Sayers (2017)

Walking with Ghosts (2017)

No Fair City: Dark Tales from Perth's Past (2017)

The Tale o the Wee Mowdie that wantit tae ken wha
keeched on his heid (2017)
SHORTLISTED FOR SCOTS CHILDREN'S BOOK OF THE YEAR 2019

Hunters: Wee Stories from the Crescent:
A Reminiscence of Perth's Hunter Crescent (2017)

A Little Book of Carol's (2018)

Flipstones (2018)

Perth: Scott's Fair City: The Fair Maid of Perth & Sir Walter Scott –
A Celebration & Guided Tour (2018)

God, Hitler, and Lord Peter Wimsey: Selected Essays, Speeches
and Articles by Dorothy L Sayers (2019)

Perth & Kinross: A Pocket Miscellany:
A Companion for Visitors and Residents (2019)

The Piper of Tobruk: Pipe Major Robert Roy, MBE, DCM(2019)

The 'Gig Docter o Athole': Dr William Irvine & The Irvine Memorial
Hospital (2019)

Afore the Highlands: The Jacobites in Perth, 1715-16 (2019)

'Where Sky and Summit Meet': Flight Over Perthshire –
A History: Tales of Pilots, Airfields, Aeronautical Feats, & War (2019)

Diverted Traffic (2020)

Authentic Democracy: An Ethical Justification of Anarchism (2020)

'If Rivers Could Sing': A Scottish River Wildlife Journey.
A Year in the Life of the River Devon as it flows through the Counties of
Perthshire, Kinross-shire & Clackmannanshire (2020)
SHORTLISTED SCOTLAND'S NATIONAL BOOK AWARDS 2021
'New Book' (Saltire Literary Awards).

A Squatter o Bairnrhymes (2020)
by Stuart A Paterson, SCOTS WRITER OF THE YEAR 2020

In a Sma Room Songbook: From the Poems by William Soutar (2020)

The Nicht Afore Christmas: the much-loved yuletide tale in Scots (2020)
SHORTLISTED FOR SCOTS CHILDREN'S BOOK OF THE YEAR 2021

Ice Cold Blood (David Millar, 2021)

The Black Watch and the Great War
(Derek Patrick and Fraser Brown (editors), 2021)

The Perth Riverside Nursery & Beyond:
A Spirit of Enterprise and Improvement
(Elspeth Bruce and Pat Kerr, 2021)

Beyond the Swelkie: A Collection of Poems & Writings to Mark the
Centenary of George Mackay Brown (1921-1996)
(Jim Mackintosh and Paul S Philippou (editors), 2021)

Dying to Live: The Remarkable True Story of Scotland's
Sickest Survivor of Covid-19
(Grant and Amanda Macintyre, 2021)

The Shanter Legacy: The Search for the Grey Mare's Tail
(Garry Stewart, 2021)

Fatal Duty: Scotland's Cop Killers, Killer Cops & More...from 1812 to 1952
(Gary Knight, 2021)

FORTHCOMING

A War of Two Halves
(Tim Barrow, Paul Beeson and Bruce Strachan, 2022)

Sweet F.A.
(Tim Barrow, Paul Beeson and Bruce Strachan, 2022)

William Soutar: Collected Poetry, Volume I
(Kirsteen McCue and Paul S Philippou (editors), 2022)

William Soutar: Collected Poetry, Volume II
(Kirsteen McCue and Paul S Philippou (editors), 2023)

Berries Fae Banes: An owersettin in Scots o the poems
bi Pino Mereu scrievit in tribute tae Hamish Henderson
(Jim Macintosh, 2022)

Perthshire 101: A Poetic Gazetteer of the Big County
(Andy Jackson (editor), 2022)

Perth City Activity Book: Exploring the Past and Present
(Felicity Graham, 2022)

The Whole Damn Town
(Hannah Ballantyne, 2022)

A British Wildlife Odyssey: In Pursuit of Britain's Wildlife Secrets
(Keith Broomfield, 2023)

All Tippermuir Books titles are available from
bookshops and online booksellers.
They can also be purchased directly
(with free postage & packing (UK only) –
minimum charges for overseas delivery) from
www.tippermuirbooks.co.uk.

Tippermuir Books Ltd can be contacted at
mail@tippermuirbooks.co.uk.